OJAI FESTIVALS ~ THE MAESTRO'S CHALLENGE

Historian & Principal Writer: ELLEN MALINO JAMES
Musicologist: JOHN HENKEN
Designer: SUZETTE CURTIS
Editor: MARY EMBREE
Managing Editor: JACQUELINE SAUNDERS

OJAI FESTIVALS, LTD.

P.O. Box 185 • 201 S. Signal Street • Ojai, California 93024
Tel: (805) 646-2094

ISBN (pbk): 0-9648970-1-6
ISBN (hdbk): 0-9648970-0-8
Library of Congress Catalog Card No. 95-71655

Printed in Hong Kong

This book is gratefully dedicated
to the memory of

LAWRENCE MORTON

T he present eminence of the Ojai Festival is due in no small part to the creative influence of Lawrence Morton. He began his association with the Festivals as program annotator in 1948 and became the artistic director in 1954. For over 30 years he served in that role or as Artistic Director Emeritus. His impeccable taste and deep musical knowledge provided programs that have won national and international acclaim.

"[He is] a man of taste and vision, of wit and erudition, an enthusiast who loves what he believes in and is fierce in condemning the sham and the superficial; he is fearless in his criticism - no sacred cows for him - and generous in his support ... Those of us who work with him and enjoy his friendship are privileged indeed." So wrote Ernest Fleischmann, executive director of the Los Angeles Philharmonic.

The long and happy relationship with Lawrence Morton remains a shining chapter in the history of the Ojai Festival.

Illustration Credits

Scenic Photography by *Bruce Ditchfield* on the following pages: Title page (hdbk), 4 - 5 (spread), 6 - 7 (spread), 8 - 9 (all), 10 - 11 (spread), 13 (top), 14 - 15 (spread), 26 (top), 28 - 29 (spread), 36, 53 (inset), Back cover.

Festival `95 Photography by *Jim Arneson*: Inside front cover, 7 (inset), 53 (top), 54 (top right), 55 (bottom), 62 - 63 (all), 64 & 65 (all), Back cover (inset).

James Abresch: 17 (middle); *Gerard Amstellem:* 61 (top right); *Marianne Barcellona:* 49 (top); *The Blakelys:* 10 (top left); Photography courtesy of *Boosey & Hawkes:* 28 (bottom left); *Paul Chinn:* 57 (bottom); Photography courtesy of *Columbia Artists Management Inc.:* 48 (top); *Peggy Ebright:* 35 (painting); *Jim Farber:* 61 (bottom right); *Foldazi:* 26 (bottom); *Betty Freeeman:* 54 (top left), 54 (bottom), 55 (top), 58 (middle), 58 (bottom), 60 (top); *Don Freeman:* 16 (drawing); *Kay Harris:* 32 (bottom left); *Hayashi Kiyotane:* 61 (left); *Robert C. Lopert:* 15 (bottom left); Photography courtesy of *Los Angeles Private Collection:* 12 (bottom); *Cathleen McIsaac:* 43 (poster art); Photography courtesy of *Ojai Festival Archives:* Front cover, 5, 11 (bottom), 12 (middle), 13 (inset), 14 (top), 14 (bottom), 15 (top right), 15 (bottom right), 18 (all), 19 (all), 20 (all), 21, 22 (all), 23 (all), 27, 29 (left), 30 (all), 31 (all), 32 (bottom), 33, 34, 37 (top), 37 (top right), 37 (bottom right), 38 (all), 39 (all), 40 (all), 41 (all), 42 (all), 43 (all), 44 (all), 49 (top left), 50 (all), 51 (all), 52 (top right), 52 (middle right), 56, 57 (top right), 58 (top left), 59 (right); *Ojai Valley Historical Society and Museum:* 17 (top), 17 (bottom); *Dave Pell:* 32 (top); *Pell-Thomas:* 28 (top left); *Pierre Petitjean:* 57 (left); *Sheldon:* 37 (bottom right); Photography courtesy of *Sony Classical (Don Hunstein):* 59 (left); *Maggie Spear:* 48 (bottom); Photography courtesy of *The Sunday Times, U.K. (Ros Drinkwater):* 60 (bottom); *Timothy Teague:* 49 (bottom), 52 (bottom); *Steven Trefonides:* 12 (top).

For information on purchasing Ojai Festival posters (late 1970s through 1991),
Please call: (805) 658-0732 or (805) 644-1376.

Acknowledgments

While every effort was made to confirm the facts in this book, Ojai Festivals, Ltd., regrets any inaccuracies or errors of omission that may have occurred. Our apologies to friends of the Festivals whom we were not able to contact or whose responses we missed at press time. We would like to extend our sincere gratitude to the following for their generous help:

- William Frank (Curator of Western Manuscripts) of the Huntington Library, San Marino, California, for permission to quote from the Ojai Festivals collection; and for waiver of publication fees.
- David Zeidberg (Head of the Department of Special Collections, University Research Library), University of California, Los Angeles, for permission to quote from Lawrence Morton, "Monday Evening Concerts," typescript of an oral history interview; and for waiver of publication fees.
- David Fry (Head of Collection Development) and Gordon Theil (Head of Library), Music Library of the University of California, Los Angeles.
- Robert L. Holman, for information about John and Helen Bauer.
- Katherine C. James of Arthur Andersen for technical assistance with data transfer.
- Betty Izant, Archivist of Ojai Festivals, Ltd.
- Arthur Morton, for generously lending his copy of the transcript of Lawrence Morton's oral history and for sharing his insights about Ojai and his late brother.

And to the following, a grateful acknowledgment for providing information, insights and memories: Eve Babitz, Mae Babitz, Mirandi Babitz, Bob Bryan, Jeff Corey, Dorothy Crawford, Ernest Fleischmann, Lukas Foss, Ralph Grierson, Fred Hall, Helen Hooker, Roger Kellaway, William Kraft, Frederick Lamb, David Lavender, Frederick Lesemann, Erna Lilliefelt, Malcolm McDowell, William Malloch, Kent Nagano, Frank Noyes, Jeannette O'Connor, David Raksin, Morris Schonbach, Eudice Shapiro, Leonard Stein, Lynford Stewart, Michael Tilson Thomas, F.B. Vanderhoef, and Elizabeth Wittausch.

The Vision

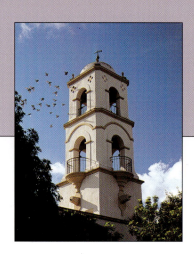

*T*he stated mission of Ojai Festivals, Ltd., which over the years has remained virtually unchanged, is to "present adventurous music at affordable prices emphasizing both contemporary composers and the discovery or rediscovery of rare or little known works by past masters. Festivals programs range from early Baroque to the avant-garde." Ojai Festivals cultivates an audience through low-cost or free concerts serving the cultural, educational and access needs of the regional population, particularly youth, through an outreach program with strong multi-cultural content.

Table of Contents

Prologue

"Ojai is a wonderfully idiosyncratic kind of occasion, a haven, a little Grail for any of us who enjoy the pilgrimage. Some of the most admired musicians of our century have been to Ojai, guaranteeing to the Festivals the highest artistic distinction. I hope that, even though our times are strange ones for the arts, Ojai would be allowed and encouraged to prosper for many years to come."

~ Ernest Fleischmann
Executive Vice President/ Managing Director,
The Los Angeles Philharmonic

For fifty years, the Ojai Valley has played host to a remarkable series of musical events which, from their beginnings in the 1940s, acquired an international reputation.

Old-timers tell stories about the Ojai Festivals — the unwritten history as they experienced it. They talk about the ancient gnarled sycamore tree around which architect Austen Pierpont designed the Festivals bowl. And of the songs and calls of wild birds which sometimes intruded on the musical sounds — except for a piece by Olivier Messiaen, performed in 1985, which included bird song in the score.

More intrusive yet was the orange train which would chug into the Ojai depot and toot its horn at some inappropriate place in the score. That locomotive almost derailed Pierre Boulez' first appearance at Ojai when it roared in just as he lifted his baton.

Those who reminisce about the early days of the Festivals spin tales about lush, romantic evenings when celebrities mingled with composers and musicians would play impromptu party songs and sometimes sing for their supper.

They remember Stravinsky's *A Soldier's Tale* performed during the second season by actors and musicians — and a decade later by puppets — and more recently again as performance art in the Peter Sellars mode. They marvel at how in all the years it never once rained on the concerts.

This music festival from the beginning was different from others taking place in and around California, such as the Music Academy of the West, founded in 1947, the same year as Ojai, or the Bach Festival at Carmel.

The music was sometimes very old and rarely performed or very new. "New" music to the wary concertgoer might mean anything without a tonal melody written after 1900. It

sometimes proved to be a "stretch" for the audience and hard as well for some of the musicians, who had to study complex scores and master new techniques.

Words like "riotous," "weird," "incomprehensible" and "primitive" began to appear in local commentary, while at the same time the more knowledgeable out-of-town critics were pronouncing these programs "courageous," "important," and in a few rare instances, "artistic triumphs."

How did this movement away from the European-dominated war-horses of the concert hall gain a foothold in the idyllic Ojai? Ojai during the 1940s was certainly open to experimentation in the arts. The innovative High Valley Theater under Alan Harkness and Iris Tree mounted productions for the Festivals during the first few years. And Beatrice Wood, already a legend in the 1920s Paris art world, drew a steady stream of visitors to her ceramics studio where she was then refining her famous pottery glazes.

Krishnamurti, who arrived in the valley in the 1920s under the wing of the Theosophists, continued to make Ojai his home, attracting visitors and disciples from among the privileged and well-educated who wintered in the valley or later settled in as permanent residents.

Others who could afford it came for their health in a climate known for its restorative sunshine and dry air. Still others had become rich in the Ventura County oil boom of the 1920s. Retired business and professional people from the East and Middle West came to the valley, already prosperous from its rich agriculture, to become growers. Along with their business abilities, they brought capital. Amid the lush orange and lemon groves they built splendid houses.

Yet old money did not easily take to new music. Where they came from, the social elite dominated orchestra boards and the programs they played, and it was commonly thought that high culture still had to originate in Europe.

By the 1940s, the American orchestral repertoire was fixed in the style of Toscanini, the colorful maestro who presided over the New York Philharmonic. His popular radio broadcasts carried music written by nineteenth-century Germans and Italians to homes in every town and city. The Bell Telephone Hour, another favorite on the airwaves, played works almost exclusively from the repertoire of Beethoven, Brahms, and Wagner. As author Joseph Horowitz said, radio created a new audience for old music.

Musical tastes in Ojai reflected these national trends. In California, attending concerts remained one of the accepted forms of pleasure for the well-to-do people of refined tastes as well as for people on the move who had not yet "arrived." Those who truly loved music wanted to bring something of the old world and of the East Coast to this new environment, to make it a place of grace and culture, to "civilize" the Californias. Elizabeth Sprague Coolidge, a winter resident in Ojai, had presented excellent chamber concerts as early as 1926.

But down in Los Angeles things were stirring. Alfred Wallenstein became the first American-born conductor to lead a major orchestra, assuming his post at the Los Angeles Philharmonic in 1944. America was just then feeling its way in the post-war cultural scene. In California especially, Americans were self-consciously proud of original American music and art and the various contributions of American-born composers.

The music milieu was further enriched by the migration

film industry. Sol Babitz was one such person. A contract musician at Twentieth Century Fox, Babitz, a violinist who also played the mandolin and viola — "anything with strings" — served as Ojai's first concert master. Babitz, a scholar of Bach and early music, also managed the personnel, contracting players for the orchestras as the need arose. Later, violist Phillip Goldberg served in this important role, and then clarinetist Julian Spear. They knew the players, their individual talents and availability, and they negotiated the fees.

Serious musicians, interested in the new music that was being talked about and composed, and who wanted to stay on the cutting edge of their profession, had few opportunities to practice their art and perform these new pieces in an intimate setting. Eudice Shapiro, the violinist, who became concertmistress of both the RKO and Paramount symphonies, tells why she came West to become a "pioneer" of new music during the 1940s: "In those days it was very difficult for a 'girl' violinist on the East Coast where I trained. The music clubs consisted of women, and they wanted a man to play."

Musicians like Shapiro and her husband, the cellist Victor Gottlieb, did not look to the Hollywood Bowl or the Los Angeles Philharmonic, both now venerable institutions dating back to the 1920s. Serious music in Los Angeles, as historian Kevin Starr has observed, had a "populist bent."

Evenings on the Roof, under the aegis of Peter Yates, was one place serious musicians could go in the 1940s. Later, its successor Monday Evening Concerts provided another such venue. All this forging ahead in the field of contemporary music belied the myth of California as a cultural wasteland.

of European composers and musicians to America which had taken place before and during the war. Many of these fine artists had taken refuge in sunny California, earning a living in Hollywood as film composers while also writing more avant-garde work on the side.

In Ojai the Festivals supported artistic freedom, so artists often worked for less; orchestras negotiated at the lower end of the union scale, and conductors often reduced their fees. They welcomed the generous rehearsal time, the perks, the parties and the attention. Most of all, in the pre-television era, they welcomed the publicity. There was Martial Singher, elegant in fedora and scarf as he stepped off the plane; and glamorous ballerina-turned-actress Vera Zorina gliding down the airport ramp at Los Angeles International. The stunning Hungarian born soprano, Magda Laszlo, was caught in the flashes of the cameras as she alighted from the Santa Fe Super Chief. There was the smiling handshake, the hug, the kiss — just like in the movies.

The musicians who were not yet soloists or stars welcomed the extra work. Most had weathered the depression years as struggling artists. Some played in orchestras organized as part of the Federal Music Project. After the war, veterans relief programs gave musicians still more work at concerts around the Southland that raised money for disabled or hospitalized soldiers.

Others came West to take studio jobs in the burgeoning

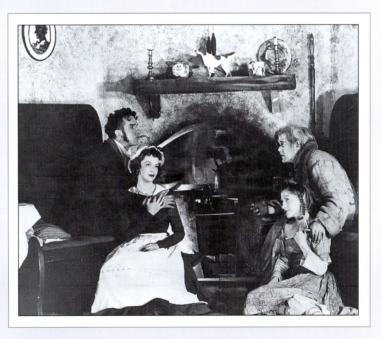

Far left: Artist Beatrice Wood, famous for her unique pottery glazes (circa 1950). Center: Ojai's famous "pink moment" provides a luminous backdrop to the luscious orange groves. Bottom right: A scene from "Cricket on the Hearth", one of the early dramatic presentations in Ojai, with Iris Tree and Woody Chambliss

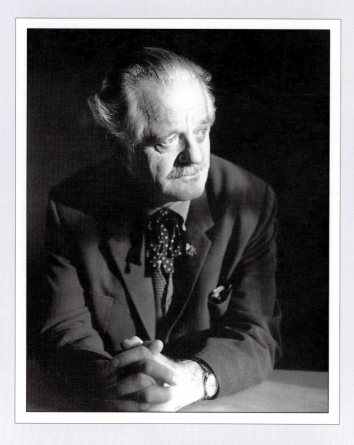

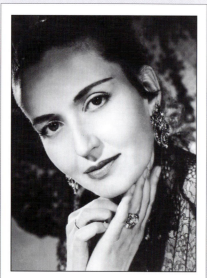

The social life alone rivalled any Greenwich Village party. The Babitzes, Sol and Mae, cooked dinners at their Hollywood home for the likes of Vera and Igor Stravinsky, Kenneth Rexroth and Lawrence Morton. Mae was also an accomplished artist who published whimsical line drawings of the events, and Vera Stravinsky designed the cover of the 1956 program book.

John and Helen Bauer were frequent guests at the Babitz home. They were an interesting couple who came from Europe and the East Coast to settle in Ojai. It was from the Bauers, who seemed to know everybody in the world, that Sol Babitz and his musician friends learned more about Ojai, this wondrous place where, for a weekend or two, they could play in an orchestra entirely of their own choosing. It was sometimes called the Ojai Festival Orchestra, the Ojai Chamber Ensemble or the Ojai Festival String Orchestra.

They would be housed and well entertained by local residents who actually knew something about music — traditional music, mostly. But these amiable people seemed willing to learn more about the new music, to try something a little different. These early years of the Festivals form the pattern for what came later. Old-timers view them through a halcyon lens, telling the tales and spinning the stories that have become part of the Festivals' lore.

The music milieu was further enriched by the migration of European composers and musicians to America.

Part 1

INSPIRATION

"There is a magic about Ojai — this is the great intangible which makes it even more beautiful than it appears on the surface... The Ojai Festivals would feature both old and new. Not just museum pieces... Unlike other festivals, we hope to begin a fresh tradition where the word Ojai will come to mean something special, unique."

~ John Bauer

THE CONDUCTORS

1947	Thor Johnson
1948	Thor Johnson, Edward Rebner
1949	Thor Johnson, Arthur William Wolf
1950	Thor Johnson
1951	William Steinberg
1952	Thor Johnson
1953	Thor Johnson, Lukas Foss

John Leopold Jergens Bauer grew up in New York City and attended Princeton as an architecture major. Traveling in Europe during summer breaks to study architecture, he also visited music festivals in Bayreuth, Munich, Vienna, Berlin, Paris and London. After Princeton, Bauer began to find his niche as a budding impresario in L.E. Behymer's office. His interest in theater and music, however, eventually took him to Washington, D.C. where he worked in promotions for the National Symphony Orchestra. He freelanced for the press department of the Metropolitan Opera and later managed the Buffalo Philharmonic.

In 1936, John Bauer was introduced to Helen Victoria Bateman by Mary MacLaren, the silent screen actress.

Helen introduced John to the Ojai Valley where her English-born parents had a home in the East End. A graduate of the Royal Conservatory of music, Helen had

taught music appreciation in English schools and, during the 1940s, wrote music reviews for the *Washington Times*. John and Helen later married and it was in 1945 that they conceived the idea of Ojai as a possible site for a festival of music and drama.

Dresden lay in ruins, along with many of the opera houses and theaters of Europe. In the United States, the Berkshire Music Festival had already begun and Cincinnati, which John Bauer knew well because he had briefly worked there, had just celebrated its silver jubilee with a music festival. Helen Bauer recalls a musician friend saying that America must now have a grown-up foreign policy and a grown-up artistic policy as well. "We decided then that when America finally comes of age, we must have a festival of chamber music because the artists needed it."

Post-war conditions in and around Ojai seemed to favor the idea of a music festival. As it was not far from Los Angeles, it had access to top musicians. Yet it offered a picturesque drive away from the city and was in a beautiful rural setting. The original staff of the Festivals consisted of Helen and John Bauer and Sallie Lou Parker, a part-time secretary, working out of the Bauers' East End home in Ojai. Bauer built a stone house as an extension to the other properties on the site. Though unfinished, it quickly became a meeting place for the Bauers' wide circle of musical and artistic friends and was featured in *Better Homes and Gardens* in 1949.

Bauer carefully cultivated a statewide committee of prominent business people, charming them into parting with their money at a time when the post-war economy did not encourage patronage of the arts. From the outset, he made the idea of the Festival something fashionable. He went to those great ladies who had room in their guest houses to host the players and the press and to give time and money and energy to this new cause.

Later, as Festivals manager, John Bauer said he could tell the difference between those who came to listen and those who came to be seen. Bauer was a society figure who was at heart a populist. He avoided social climbers and attracted music lovers.

Among the Ojai women whose appreciation of serious music went far beyond the merely casual were the Misses Robertson: Ruth, Alice, and Helen of the East End; Mrs. Florence Gates Baldwin of Rancho Matilija and San

He went to those great ladies who had room in their guest houses to host the players and the press and could give time, money and energy to this new cause.

14

Marino; Mrs. George French Porter, sister of the French composer Marcelle de Manziarly, whose work was performed at the 1950 Festival; Mrs. Harry Gorham and her daughter, the redoubtable Constance Rogers Wash; and Mrs. Morgan Baker.

Connie Wash at her family manse, *Journey's End*, headed up that most important hospitality committee. Margie Baker, Margaret Reimer, Mary Harmon and Helen Robertson were among those who started the Festivals' thrift shop, still a going concern today.

The first concert, held May 4, 1947, featured baritone Martial Singher with Paul Ulanowsky at the piano, assisted by flutist Doriot Anthony and the cellist Victor Gottlieb, in a recital covering repertoire from Rameau to Ravel. The negotiations for Singher were not easy. Bauer, who was a personal friend of the baritone, first appealed to Singher's vanity. He would be the first artist ever to appear in Ojai. It was also Singher's first concert in California.

Then Bauer had to convince Singher's agency, L.E. Behymer (where Bauer had once worked) that the Ojai Festival, which no one had ever heard of, was real, quite respectable and solvent. Singher got permission to reduce his fee and confided to Bauer that the publicity value of his appearance, the high standards of the artistry, and the social aspects of his visit to Ojai would more than compensate for the lower fee.

The first concert and two other events were held over the course of three weeks in May and June at the Nordhoff High School auditorium (now Matilija Junior High School). As the Nordhoff auditorium only seated four hundred, those who couldn't get in stood outside and watched through the windows. After each performance, subscribers were invited to meet the artists at the Ojai Valley Inn for a buffet. Helen Bauer wrote the program notes for the first concert — without attribution.

The first three seasons brought dramatic performances by the High Valley Theater (*Macbeth,* Iris Tree's *Second Wind* and *Frankie and Johnny,* among others). In these early days, the Festivals put as much emphasis on drama as on music. John Bauer claimed that the players were the

Far left and center: John Bauer and his Ojai estate in the East End. Left: Connie Wash, an early supporter of the Festivals and a frequent hostess of many artists over the years. Above: Bruno Walter and Delia Reinhardt enjoy the view of the Ojai Valley from the home of Connie Wash.

Top right: A publicity photo showing baritone Martial Singher in an imposing opera costume. Far right: Iris Tree and Ford Rainey in an Ojai performance of "Macbeth."

In the illustration, handwritten labels read:
- JOSEPH SCHUSTER PLAYING A BEETHOVEN SONATA
- THOR JOHNSON CONDUCTS
- SHURA CHERKASSKY performing the world premiere of Keller's Concerto
- INTERMISSION —
- BRUNETTA MAZZOLINI SINGS MOZART'S GREAT MASS IN C MINOR
- MEMBERS OF THE JUILLIARD STRING QUARTET OPERATE ON A CELLO DURING A REHEARSAL

only professional repertory company in California: "The High Valley Theater may be likened to those permanent theatrical organizations in Europe which have maintained and developed the finest traditions of the theater." Director Alan Harkness had trained under Michael Chekhov in England.

Bauer also called for a new form of theater: "chamber opera." He proposed specially commissioned works more indigenous to the new world than the old with its "grand" opera. He also planned to feature dance in all its forms — from primitive to traditional and contemporary. In time, the plays and dramas would fall by the wayside in favor of all-music programs with some occasional dance.

Only at the end of this first concert series did Bauer issue a plan for the Festivals and begin work on incorporating them into a non-profit organization. He wanted the 1949 season to mark the official launching of Ojai Festivals, Ltd., to coincide with the upcoming California Centennial Celebration.

The original plan was to hold eight festivals, each of six days' duration. All this would be housed in a special festival playhouse, to be built on a site in Ojai. Seating only about 1200, it would not hold large audiences. "No attempt will be made to have record crowds attend. The intimate approach will be stressed — intimate without being so small that the plan becomes financially impossi-

The New York Times commissioned a sketch of the Festivals in 1949 by artist Don Freeman.

ble." The playhouse was never built, but the concept that Bauer elaborated in the original mission statement has survived:

"At a time when a war-torn world is endeavoring to rehabilitate itself and find the way to build an enduring peace, it becomes even more evident that music and the arts are human blessings which rise above man-made barriers of nationalism and prejudice. Though there was little opportunity during the war for much artistic creation, most countries did wonders in keeping alive their traditions of music, drama and art. Almost as soon as the fighting ceased there was evident a passionate desire on the part of all peoples to rebuild their cultural life among the physical ruins around them. While the U.S. is 'young and fresh,' it is too often dominated by outmoded artistic conventions imported from Europe... More and more the West will tend to offer its own contribution to the intellectual life of the country — and to the world. People already know California as a land of varied scenery and agreeable climate. They will come to know it as an artistic center as well through the contribution that the Ojai Festivals will make."

Bauer clearly expected outsiders, not people from Ojai, to make up the largest proportion of attendees. He stressed the accessibility by road, rail and air from Los Angeles, Santa Barbara and San Francisco with "ample accommodation in private homes and in the many existing hotels."

Along with Bauer, the two other signatories of the original incorporation papers were Noel Sullivan of Carmel and San Francisco, noted art and music patron and nephew of the late Senator James Phelan; and Eugene Eckerle of Cincinnati, music patron and aluminum industry magnate.

Through Eckerle and Bauer, who had done public relations for the Cincinnati summer opera, the Festival established a working relationship with the young American conductor of the Cincinnati Symphony, Thor Johnson, who would lead the artists for six of the first seven Festival seasons. Johnson was a protégé of Serge Koussevitzky.

The years 1947-51 launched a series of elegant patrons' recitals and readings by Hollywood personalities such as Charles Laughton in 1949. Irene Dunne arranged for the use of the Ojai Valley Inn of which she was part owner; and actors Hurd Hatfield and Joel McCrea were listed in the programs as patrons.

This Hollywood connection did not escape the notice of Hedda Hopper, who in 1947 gave a prominent mention to the Festivals in her *Los Angeles Times* column. The *New York Times* commissioned a sketch of the Festivals in 1949 by artist Don Freeman which ran on the front page of their Arts and Entertainment section. In the spring of 1949, the Ojai Festival was also featured as the Auto Club's "Trip of the Week." And in newspapers all over the

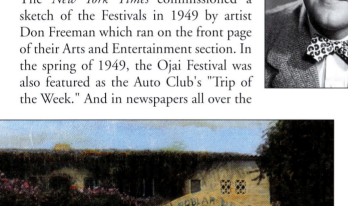

country, Ojai was featured as a "mecca" for music lovers.

This extraordinary publicity had to do with Bauer's own press releases and the manner in which he presented plans to the editors as a fait accompli when in fact they were sometimes just plans. In the summer of 1951 Bauer went to Salzburg to enter Ojai in an international Olympiad of Festivals.

Despite the apparent success of these first years, however, retrenchment was already in the air by 1949 when the Board had to cut back the two-weekend series of concerts to just one weekend, as it is today. Wilfred Rothschild, who was chairman of the Board, explained why: the deficits had to be made up personally by board members. A group of Festival "friends" from Los Angeles proved to be indispensable financially. Los Angeles continues to be an important source of Festival patrons, comprising more than 60% of the audience each year.

The Board's policy of retrenchment that year created certain logistical problems for the musicians. With a shortened schedule of concerts, there were simply too many of them. In one concert, conductor Thor Johnson and the chamber orchestra played little more than accompaniments to the soloists. Among these were famed pianist Shura Cherkassky, who performed the world premiere of a new piano concerto by Homer Keller. Keller was a local composer from Ventura County whose work had received little recognition in this country.

The year 1950 marked the first time rehearsals were held in Ojai, and subscribers were invited to attend in the elegant lobby of the old Foothills Hotel, which the Festivals took over to house and feed the musicians. The powerful Musicians Union encouraged members of the local to play at Ojai. According to a union official, the best musicians wanted to be there because they had heard that Ojai was becoming more like Salzburg, even though Ojai did not have the advantage of being the birthplace or home of a famous musical figure.

There was much anticipation in the Valley before the 1950 concerts. Helen Hooker recalls that, when she and her husband Alan had just opened the Ranch House restaurant, John and Helen Bauer came running over to

Bottom left: The El Roblar Hotel, which later became The Oaks Resort. Center: Thor Johnson, who was principal conductor at six of the first seven festivals. Top right: The Foothills Hotel, now no more, which was used to house musicians and for rehearsals and receptions.

alert them to the crowds that would be coming up for the Festival. "They filled our place those first years. From then on, Alan and I had the same seats under the branch of that tree."

On Friday evening, May 26, 1950, a lieder recital was scheduled to take place with Bruno Walter at the piano accompanying soprano Delia Reinhardt. They would be assisted by the husband and wife team of Nikolai and Joanna Graudan on cello and piano. Bauer had originally proposed to Walter in February of that year an all-Mahler Festival which Walter pronounced "beyond human capacities." In any event, this more modest Bruno Walter concert never took place. Two hours before the concert, Madame Reinhardt announced that she was suffering from laryngitis. The Graudans stepped in on short notice to fill the gap. For the improvised portion of their program, the Graudans played popular favorites — sonatas by Beethoven and Debussy.

Newspaper deadlines being what they were in those days, several papers, especially the evening ones, reported that this eagerly awaited concert had actually taken place. Although Walter had performed in Ojai earlier that year at a private patrons' concert, to this day people refer to the time Bruno Walter played at the Ojai Festival and that lady sang.

Above: Hungarian pianist Lili Kraus plays at the 1951 Festival. Top center: Audience and orchestra await the conductor on a balmy afternoon in the 1950s. Top right: Pianist Lili Kraus and Ingolf Dahl take a bow at the 1951 Festival. Dahl also played piano that year in Ojai. Bottom right: Guest conductor and pianist Lukas Foss, captured in a pensive mood.

One of the star performers for the 1951 concerts, to be conducted by William Steinberg, had already arrived in the Valley that spring. Hungarian-born pianist Lili Kraus entertained patrons with a program of Bach, Mozart, Beethoven, Schubert, and *Peasant Songs and Dances* by her former teacher and favorite composer, Bela Bartók.

Kraus and her husband, Dr. Otto Mandl, were guests of the sisters Robertson. A war refugee, Kraus was widely known in this country because of her best selling pre-war recordings. Made stateless after the war, Kraus and her family were eventually offered citizenship by New Zealand. But for a time during the 1950s, she considered Ojai her second home. She returned often to visit the Happy Valley School, to perform for Festivals patrons at the Krotona Institute, and to play again at the 1957 Festival.

Bauer was sometimes criticized for not programming enough new music, but the 1951 season included the world premiere, commissioned by the Festivals through the Huntington Hartford Foundation, of Alexei Haieff's String Quartet. Program notes were written by Lawrence Morton, a critic and champion of new music who was about to make his mark with Monday Evening Concerts in Los Angeles. Morton wrote that Haieff's piece was the kind you had to hear three or four times before you could make up your

complained: "though an audience may think it is charmed, it is really distracted by the waving of branches in the breeze, the movement of clouds, the flickering of sunlight on a lawn, or spiders crawling up a neighbor's sleeve. I love nature as much as the next fellow but I take it straight; and I like my music straight."

Morton also objected to what he perceived to be a lowering of standards in repertoire. He called the Mendelssohn Violin Concerto a virtuoso war horse, not suitable for festivals. He regretted the "abandonment of this spirit of adventure" that had lead the Festivals in former years to take chances with music by Schoenberg, Haieff, Copland, and Hindemith.

"The purpose of a festival is not to duplicate but to surpass the activities of the regular season, not to be self-supporting but to nourish the arts. One problem solved, another has arisen — namely the problem of maintaining those artistic standards which are the only excuse for having a festival at all."

Yet the highly successful season that followed brought accolades for its courage. The program began with a piece that brought the house down, but not as expected, when the Walden Quartet gave the first West Coast performance of Elliott Carter's String Quartet (No. 1) composed only two years earlier. The atonal music stirred up such a furor that Bauer handed out mimeographed copies of Virgil Thomson's review of its New York premiere in hopes of convincing the audience that they had indeed heard a great work.

The Carter performance was followed the next day by a program of Boccherini, Bartók, and Bruch — the three B's, as someone said, but not the traditional ones. A highlight of the Festival was the appearance of sensational wunderkind Lukas Foss as guest conductor and pianist in the first West Coast performance of his *Parable of Death*, narrated by Vera Zorina. (Foss recalled recently that he had asked Zorina, who had danced for Balanchine, to narrate that piece when it first premiered on the East Coast; and so he

mind about its meaning and importance.

The 1952 program book included, for the first time, advertisements from local merchants, tastefully done with Ojai history and photos, but ads nonetheless. Lawrence Morton, writing in the July 1952 issue of the liberal magazine *Frontier* under the heading "Dark Clouds Over Ojai," said, "Ojai would be unique if it did not have financial problems. Until this year those problems have remained hidden... For the first time the Festival's financial slip has been allowed to show."

Thor Johnson returned for his fifth season in 1952, which was notable for the appearance of celebrated soprano Rose Bampton and a theater event with Judith Anderson. Anderson was familiar to Ojai audiences because she had toured with the Broadway production of Robinson Jeffers' *Medea*. Jeffers had prepared a reading version especially for Ojai and Anderson dedicated her performance to him "since the musicians... dedicate their performances to the great composers."

In 1952, the concerts were first moved to Libbey Park, and the increased seating permitted the Festivals to reduce ticket prices. But Morton intensely disliked the change in venue. He

wanted her to fly out for the Ojai performance.) A reception at the El Roblar hotel following this performance was mobbed.

Foss would remain popular with Ojai audiences. He returned to conduct for six more seasons, spanning three remarkable decades from 1961 through 1987.

Before Bauer's last season in 1953, he restated the goals of the Festivals that he had laid out in his prospectus of 1947. In a flyer in March 1952, he wrote: "The period of trial and error must now come to an end... [we must] profit by our errors and capitalize on our successes."

In November 1953, the Festivals' Board announced it would not be renewing Bauer's appointment as general manager and appointed instead Lawrence Morton as artistic director. Bauer noted that he had been reelected to the Board for a new term of three years ending in 1956 — and so he had. But by 1954, his name was gone from the program and an era had ended.

Former *Los Angeles Times* critic, Albert Goldberg, said in a 1983 interview that Bauer was a "visionary" who could "charm his way through a brick wall." Goldberg recalled, "Bauer created the atmosphere and the name. He wanted Ojai to become the Bayreuth of America." Goldberg, who retired from the *Times* in 1965, continued his visits to the Ojai as critic emeritus until his death in 1990.

By 1954 Ojai had carved out a place in the literature of festivals. Locally, as Helen Bauer had predicted in 1946, its popularity was due to the growth that would bring visitors to the county and new residents as well. And in Europe, tourist magazines now referred to Ojai as "The California Salzburg."

~ Ellen Malino James

Top: Igor Stravinsky emerges from the Ojai "Green Room" tent, mid-1950s. Above: William Steinberg, who was the principal conductor for the 1951 season. Opposite: Robert Craft and Franz Waxman watch Stravinsky and Lawrence Morton confer, circa 1955.

Music Notes

John Henken

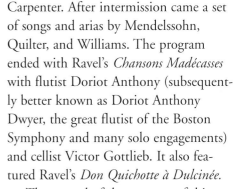

ALTHOUGH there was much about the Ojai Festival in its early years that would seem unfamiliar to most Festival veterans today, its musical profile was clearly defined from the very beginning. An enlightened eclecticism, a sense that musical adventure should be fun and inspiring rather than hard duty, and a confident, international outlook that grew from secure local roots characterized the new project.

Technically, Festival founders considered the events of 1947 preliminaries, with the first of the official Ojai Festivals scheduled for May-June 1949. Success was immediate, however, and the Ojai Festival has ever since counted its origin from May 4, 1947 with a recital by the great French baritone Martial Singher. The cautious prediction in the program booklet that "this afternoon's song recital may well prove an historic moment" has proven to be true.

Born in 1904, Singher came to the United States in 1941 and was an established artist at the Metropolitan Opera in New York when Ojai brought him across the country for his first performance in California. (He would return the following year, eventually to move permanently to Santa Barbara, where he was a force for many years.) Singher's program, accompanied by pianist Paul Ulanowsky, was utterly characteristic, both of the man and of the Ojai ideal. It began with a French Baroque set — at a time when this was not popular repertory — followed by a group of serenades from Schubert, Berlioz, Gounod, Brahms, and

THOR JOHNSON

Carpenter. After intermission came a set of songs and arias by Mendelssohn, Quilter, and Williams. The program ended with Ravel's *Chansons Madécasses* with flutist Doriot Anthony (subsequently better known as Doriot Anthony Dwyer, the great flutist of the Boston Symphony and many solo engagements) and cellist Victor Gottlieb. It also featured Ravel's *Don Quichotte à Dulcinée.*

The second of three events of this "preliminary" season was a staging of Shakespeare's *Macbeth* on May 18, 1947. The third was the debut of the Ojai Festival Chamber Orchestra on June 15. Conducting the ensemble was Thor Johnson, the newly appointed conductor of the Cincinnati Symphony, in his California debut. A student of Felix Weingartner, Bruno Walter, and Serge Koussevitzky, among others, Johnson had impressive artistic and organizational credentials, having founded the Little Symphony of Ann Arbor and the Asheville Mozart Festival while teaching at the University of Michigan. After military service in World War II, he became conductor of the Juilliard Orchestra and made guest appearances with the New York Philharmonic, the Boston Symphony, the Chicago Symphony, and the Philadelphia Orchestra, in addition to the Cincinnati Symphony.

The orchestra Thor Johnson had at his disposal was a solid one, 32 strong, with many musicians who would be pillars of the southern California music

Right: Robert Craft, who enjoyed a close relationship with Stravinsky, and conducted at Ojai during the 1950s. Below: Lawrence Morton and Igor Stravinsky enjoyed a relationship of comaraderie and respect. Bottom right: A youthful picture of the Juilliard Quartet, who performed in Ojai during the first decade.

Johnson would return as principal conductor and the untitled music director every year except one through 1953. The exception was 1951, when William Steinberg was the conductor. That season, the Festivals' fifth, was a significant one, including the Festivals' first children's concerts. It boasted four programs by the Festival Chamber Orchestra, with soloists including violinist Szymon Goldberg, pianist Lili Kraus, and the Stanford University Chorus. There was also a Mozart program for woodwinds and recitals by Goldberg and Kraus.

The 1951 season also included a concert by the American Art Quartet, led by violinst Eudice Shapiro, honoring the 25th anniversary of the Ojai Valley Festival of Chamber Music sponsored by the great arts patroness Elizabeth Sprague Coolidge. The program featured the world premiere of Alexei Haieff's First String Quartet, a Festivals commission, and the West Coast premiere of Copland's year-old Quartet for Piano and Strings with Ingolf Dahl the pianist, a work commissioned by the Elizabeth Sprague Coolidge Foundation.

Completing the 1951 Festival schedule were two programs from the influen-

scene, such as concertmaster Sol Babitz, French hornist Sinclair Lott, cellist Mary Louise Zeyen, and bassoonist Don Christlieb.

The program Johnson assigned his charges began with a Concerto in D for viols, rather tenuously ascribed to C.P.E. Bach and arranged for small orchestra by Maximilian Steinberg. It continued with Schubert's Symphony No. 5 in B-flat, followed after intermission by the California premiere of the 1942 Symphony for Chamber Orchestra by Juilliard faculty composer William Bergsma. To close came another recent work, the antic *Divertissement* Ibert extracted from his score for René Clair's farcical film, *Le chapeau de paille d'Italie*.

With this, the Ojai Festival was well and truly established artistically. Thor

tial Lester Horton Dancers, capped by the first performances of Horton's "choreodrama" *Medea*, to an original score by Audree Covington.

In 1954 Lawrence Morton became artistic director of the Ojai Festival — the first to be accorded that title officially. Although the Festival would bear the stamp of his sophisticated musical intelligence and wide-ranging interests, he worked no revolution — the Festival was cast in a compatibly "Mortonian" mold from the beginning. The indefatigable musicologist-impresario was first formally associated with the Ojai Festival as the program annotator in 1948.

Born in Duluth, Minnesota, in 1904, Morton became a professional musician while still in his teens, playing organ for silent movies. In the early 1930s he chanced upon two works — by two composers who would play a significant role in the Ojai story — which altered his musical focus: Copland's Piano Variations and Stravinsky's *Symphony of Psalms*. Moving to California, he found his way to Evenings on the Roof, where he gradually became involved enough to succeed Peter Yates at the end of the 1953/54 season. Under Morton, the series went on to even greater fame as Monday Evening Concerts.

For the first three seasons of his Festival tenure, Morton chose Robert Craft, Stravinsky's increasingly important right hand, as the principal conductor. This, of course, had an effect on the programming. Stravinsky had been featured at Ojai as early as 1948, when a performance of *Histoire du soldat* (A Soldier's Tale) — billed as the premiere of the final version, with additional dialogue from Ramuz — opened the season. This work, in its combination of music and drama, economy and power, would become a representative hallmark of the Festivals.

Morton had already begun what was

to be a long and happy relationship with Stravinsky when he took over both Monday Evening Concerts and the Ojai Festivals. Stravinsky himself was there with Craft to conduct some of his own works in 1955 and 1956. His arrangement of Bach's Chorale and Variations on "Von Himmel hoch", which had its world premiere at the Festival in 1956, did not come easily. In February 1956 he wrote to Nadia Boulanger that "The Bach Variations are taking more time than I had anticipated; I am going to have Bob [Craft] conduct them in May at the Ojai Festival, when I conduct my *Noces*," and it was not until Easter that he finally had the work finished and sent to his publisher.

Among the highlights of the Festivals' first decade was Shura Cherkassky playing the world premiere in 1949 of the Ojai-commissioned Piano Concerto by Homer Keller (an Oxnard native whose First Symphony won the Henry Hadley Award in 1940 and was performed by the New York Philharmonic). Other artists included Lukas Foss, Marilyn Horne, Theodore Uppman, the Hollywood String Quartet, the Juilliard String Quartet, the Lichine Ballet, and the San Francisco Ballet. The Festivals also commissioned works from Peter Jona Korn and Marcelle de Manziarly to go with an imposing list of Bartók, Dallapiccola, Stravinsky, and other contemporaries, but in sheer number of performances Mozart was by far the dominant composer, distantly followed by Beethoven and Bach.

Opposite and bottom left: Musicians rehearsed wherever they could find a quiet moment, backstage or in the park.

THE ARCHIVES
PART 1 & 2

FIRST FESTIVAL
May 4 through June 15, 1947
Conductor: Thor Johnson
Festival Coordinator: John Bauer
Venue: Nordhoff Auditorium*
Performers: Ojai Festival Chamber Orchestra
Doriot Anthony - flute
Victor Gottlieb - cello
Martial Singher - baritone
Paul Ulanowsky - piano

SECOND FESTIVAL
May 21 - 23, and May 28-30, 1948
Conductors: Thor Johnson, Edward Rebner
Festival Coordinator: John Bauer
Venue: Nordhoff Auditorium*
Performers: Ojai Festival Chamber Orchestra
San Francisco String Quartet
Martial Singher - baritone
Paul Ulanowsky - piano

THIRD FESTIVAL
May 27-29, 1949
Conductors: Thor Johnson, Arthur William Wolf
Managing Director: John Bauer
Venue: Nordhoff Auditorium*
Performers: Ojai Festival Chamber Orchestra
Ojai Festival Bach Chorus and Orchestra
Juilliard String Quartet
Shura Cherkassky - piano
Joseph Schuster - cello

FOURTH FESTIVAL
May 26-30, 1950
Conductor: Thor Johnson
Managing Director: John Bauer
Venue: Nordhoff Auditorium*
Performers: Ojai Festival Chamber Orchestra
American Art Quartet
Stanford University Chorus
Nikolai and Joanna Graudan, cello and piano
Jascha Veissi, viola

FIFTH FESTIVAL
May 25-30, 1951
Conductor: William Steinberg
Managing Director: John Bauer
Venues: Nordhoff Auditorium*, Community Church,
Art Center Theatre, Ventura Jr. College Auditorium
Performers: Ojai Festival Chamber Orchestra
American Art Quartet
Lester Horton Dancers
Los Angeles Woodwinds
Stanford University Chorus
Ingolf Dahl - piano
Szymon Goldberg - violin
Joanna and Nikolai Graudan - piano and cello
Lili Kraus - piano
Mitchell Lurie - clarinet
Jascha Veissi, viola

SIXTH FESTIVAL
May 30-31, June 1, 1952
Conductor: Thor Johnson
Managing Director: John Bauer
Venues: Nordhoff Auditorium* (3 concerts),
Ojai Civic Center Park (2 concerts)
Performers: Ojai Festival Chamber Orchestra
Judith Anderson - actress
Rose Bampton - soprano
Szymon Goldberg - violin.
Nikolai and Joanna Graudan - cello and piano

SEVENTH FESTIVAL
May 22 - 24, 1953
Conductors: Thor Johnson, Lukas Foss
Managing Director: John Bauer
Venues: Nordhoff Auditorium* (3 concerts),
Civic Center Park (2 concerts), Art Center Theatre
Performers: Ojai Festival Orchestra
Pomona College Glee Clubs
Walden Quartet
Joseph Eger - horn
Lukas Foss - piano
James Schwabacher - tenor
Vera Zorina - narrator

EIGHTH FESTIVAL
May 21 - 23, 1954
Conductor: Robert Craft
John Bauer resigned as Managing Director, replaced by
Lawrence Morton as Artistic Director
Venue: Nordhoff Auditorium* (4 concerts),
Civic Center Park (1 concert)
Performers: Ojai Festival String Orchestra
Hollywood String Quartet
Lichine Ballet with Tatiana Riabouchinska
Los Angeles Wood Winds
Pomona College Glee Clubs
Ingolf Dahl and Shibley Boyes - piano four-hands
Lukas Foss - piano
Nan Merriman - mezzo-soprano
Eudice Shapiro - violin

NINTH FESTIVAL
May 20 - 22, 1955
Conductors: Robert Craft, Igor Stravinsky
Artistic Director: Lawrence Morton
Venues: Nordhoff Auditorium* (3 concerts), Civic Center Park
(2 concerts), Ventura High School Auditorium
(2 children's concerts)
Performers: Ojai Festival Chamber Orchestra
Pomona College Glee Clubs
San Francisco Ballet Company
Phyllis Althof - soprano
Appleton and Field - duo-pianists
Marilyn Horne - soprano
Joseph Schuster - cello
Eudice Shapiro - violin

TENTH FESTIVAL
May 25 - 27, 1956
Conductors: Robert Craft, Igor Stravinsky
Artistic Director: Lawrence Morton
Venues: Nordhoff Auditorium* (2 concerts),
Civic Center Park (3 concerts),
Ventura High School Auditorium (2 children's concerts)
Performers: Ojai Festival Orchestra
The American Chamber Players
Pomona College Glee Clubs
Marilyn Horne - soprano
Magda Laszlo - soprano

ELEVENTH FESTIVAL
May 24 - 26, 1957
Conductors: Aaron Copland, Ingolf Dahl
Artistic Director: Lawrence Morton
Venues : Nordhoff Auditorium* (2 concerts),
Civic Center Park Bowl (3 concerts)
Performers: Ojai Festival Orchestra and Chamber Ensemble
Ojai Festival Chorus
Fine Arts Wind Players
Lili Kraus - piano
Sinclair Lott - horn
Mitchell Lurie - clarinet

Margery MacKay - mezzo-soprano
Richard Robinson - tenor

TWELFTH FESTIVAL
May 23 - 25, 1958
Conductor: Aaron Copland
Artistic Director: Lawrence Morton
Venues: Nordhoff Auditorium* (2 concerts),
Civic Center Park Bowl (3 concerts), (All late afternoon con-
certs, since lighting was not yet available for night concerts.)
Performers: Ojai Festival Symphony Orchestra
        Ventura College Concert Chorale and
            Chamber Singers
        The Immaculate Heart Trio
        Phyllis Althof Brill - soprano
        Grace Bumbry, mezzo-soprano
        Bert Gassman - oboe
        Robert Ryan - narrator
        Leo Smit - piano
        Dorothy Wade - violin

THIRTEENTH FESTIVAL
May 22 - 24, 1959
Conductor: Robert Craft
Artistic Director: Lawrence Morton
Venues: Nordhoff Auditorium* (3 concerts),
Civic Center Park (2 concerts)
Performers: Ojai Festival Orchestra
        The Gregg Smith Singers
        The Paganini Quartet
        Eva Gustavson - contralto
        Natasha Litvin - piano
        Margery MacKay - mezzo-soprano
        Grace-Lynne Martin - soprano
        Robert Oliver - bass
        Dorothy Remsen - harp
        Richard Robinson - tenor

FOURTEENTH FESTIVAL
May 21 - 28, May 28 - 30, 1960
Conductor: Henri Temianka
Artistic Advisor: Franklin Lacey (Lawrence Morton
was in Paris on a Guggenheim Fellowship).
Venues: Festival Bowl in Civic Center Park.
Performers: Anna Maria Alberghetti and Family
        Lotte Goslar and Company
        The Temianka Little Symphony
        Dorothy Kirsten - soprano
        Luboschutz and Nemenoff - duo-pianists
        John Raitt - baritone

FIFTEENTH FESTIVAL
May 19 - 21, 1961
Conductor: Lukas Foss
Festival Coordinator: Richard Duffalo
Performers: Ojai Festival Orchestra
        Roger Wagner Chorale
        The Improvisation Chamber Ensemble
        Lenox Quartet
        The Previn-Manne-Mitchell Trio
        Howard Chitjian - baritone
        Lukas Foss -piano
        Maurita Phillips - soprano
        André Previn - piano
        Richard Robinson - tenor
        Eudice Shapiro - violin
        Leo Smit - piano
        James Tippey - bass

SIXTEENTH FESTIVAL
May 18 - 20, 1962
Conductor: Lukas Foss
Guest composer/conductor: Luciano Berio

Festival Coordinator: Richard Duffalo
Performers: Ojai Festival Orchestra
        The Gregg Smith Singers
        Roger Wagner Chorale
        Cathy Berberian - mezzo-soprano
        Eric Dolphy - flute
        Lukas Foss - piano
        Margery MacKay - mezzo-soprano
        Marni Nixon - soprano
        André Previn - piano
        Leo Smit - piano
        Mallory Walker - tenor

SEVENTEENTH FESTIVAL
May 24-26, 1963
Conductors: Lukas Foss, Leonard Stein, Richard Duffalo
Guest composer/conductor: Mauricio Kagel
Festival Coordinator: Richard Duffalo
Performers: Ojai Festival Orchestra
        The Gregg Smith Singers
        The Lilliputian Players
        Combined concert choirs of UCLA, USC
            and St. Charles Mens and Boys Choir
        Vocal Arts Ensemble
        Ernst Krenek - piano
        Lui Tsun-Yuen - pipa
        Lui Hung - Chinese classical dancer
        Sanford Schonbach - viola
        Eudice Shapiro - violin
        Leonard Stein - piano

EIGHTEENTH FESTIVAL
May 29-31, 1964
Conductor: Ingolf Dahl
Festival Manager: Frederick Lesemann
Performers: Ojai Festival Orchestra
        Berkeley Chamber Singers
        Los Angeles String Quartet
        Pomona College Glee Clubs
        USC Concert Choir
        Fred Hemke - saxophone
        Eudice Shapiro - violin
        Lillian Steuber - piano

NINETEENTH FESTIVAL
May 21-23, 1965
Conductors: Ingolf Dahl, Karl Kohn
Production Manager: Frederick Lesemann
Performers: Ojai Festival Orchestra
        Los Angeles String Quartet
        Los Angeles Woodwinds
        Trojan String Quartet
        USC Concert Choir
        Alice Ehlers & Malcolm Hamilton - harpsichordists
        Laurence Lesser - cello
        Grace-Lynne Martin - soprano
        Eudice Shapiro - violin
        Michael Tilson Thomas - piano

TWENTIETH FESTIVAL
May 20-22, 1966
Conductor: Ingolf Dahl, Roger Wagner
Production Manager: Frederick Lesemann
Performers: Ojai Festival Orchestra
        Boston Symphony Chamber Players
        UCLA Concert Choir
        UCSB Chamber Singers
        The William Hall Chorale
        Doriot Anthony Dwyer - flute
        Eudice Shapiro - violin
        Leo Smit - piano
        Michael Tilson Thomas - piano
*Nordoff Auditorium was located at what is now Matilija Junior High School.

25

THE SETTING

Perhaps it is the very word "valley" that conjures associations of a mythical place suspended between heaven and earth, hospitable to humans, protected by the gods and set apart by virtue of its perimeters from the chaos of the borderlands beyond. Certainly the Ojai Valley embodies these physical properties and the harmony of nature has in turn evoked a harmony of spirit enjoyed by all who live or visit here. Frank Capra transformed Ojai into Shangri-La for his 1937 film *Lost Horizon,* and it continues to be a refuge and a wellspring of regeneration for the harried folks from Los Angeles that come to slow down and be refreshed.

Famous for its population of creative artists, writers, painters and thespians, Ojai has also provided an atmosphere of spaciousness and transformation for many meditative and contemplative groups that have made the Valley their spiritual home.

Until 1916, Ojai was called Nordhoff, after Charles Nordhoff, the writer who had first publicized the place. That year the town chose to revert to the earlier name of "Ojai", given by the Chumash Indians who settled here some one thousand years ago. To this day, it is undecided whether "Ojai" means nest or moon, but in either case, the essentially nurturing atmosphere of the Valley is invoked. In 1917, Edward Drummond Libbey, the Toledo industrialist who first made Ojai fashionable as a winter resort, donated to the city the land that became Civic Center Park, later renamed Libbey Park.

In Libbey Park today, faint echoes still exist of earlier times when Ojai functioned as the sacred ground of peace for the restless tribes in Southern California. The ancient arched sycamore tree in the heart of the Libbey Bowl stands as a sentinel to the days when the Chumash would bend over a young tree and fasten its top in the earth to mark a sacred spot. Long years ago, the Libbey Bowl sycamore was known as the "Peace Tree" and the "Marriage Tree". It was used ceremonially in rites of union or peace treaty. Today it still marks a spot where inspiration and creativity flourish, drawing 5,000 people a year to experience the melding of mind, music and nature at the Ojai Festival.

The serene vistas of the Ojai Valley well deserve the association with Shangri-La. Below, the ancient sycamore located in the Libbey Bowl.

Information on the Chumash based on a 1953 article by George T. Channing.

Part 2

THE FINE LINE

*"To have lived one's life in music and through music, with the other
arts and literature, is to have enjoyed the companionship of the best minds and
noblest spirits that have justified mankind's existence on this earth."*

~ Lawrence Morton

THE CONDUCTORS

1954 Robert Craft	1962 Lukas Foss, Luciano Berio,
1955 Robert Craft and Igor Stravinsky	André Previn, Gunther Schuller,
1956 Robert Craft and Igor Stravinsky	Leo Smit, Roger Wagner
1957 Aaron Copland and Ingolf Dahl,	1963 Lukas Foss, Richard Duffalo,
Owen Brady	Mauricio Kagel, Leonard Stein
1958 Aaron Copland	1964 Ingolf Dahl
1959 Robert Craft	1965 Ingolf Dahl
1960 Henri Temianka	1966 Ingolf Dahl
1961 Lukas Foss	

Lawrence Morton began writing music criticism during the late 1930s when he arrived in Los Angeles from his native Minnesota and became involved with a circle of local musicians who attended rooftop concerts at the Los Angeles home of Peter Yates. After Yates resigned as director of Evenings on the Roof in 1952, Morton eventually succeeded him, naming the new series Monday Evening Concerts, which found a home in 1965 at the Leo S. Bing Theater of the Los Angeles County Museum of Art. At that time, Morton also became the curator of music at the Museum.

Elsewhere, new conductors and composers were emerging. Leonard Bernstein, upon arriving at the New York Philharmonic in the late 1950s, described the repertoire there as one that began with Mozart and ended with Mahler.

Elliott Carter recalled how at the Boston Symphony Koussevitzky would inflict Brahms on a restless audience (or at least that was Carter's perception). New ideas were

Luka Foss conducting orchestra and soloists in 1961.

Above: Stravinsky and Robert Craft consult on a score (1956). Right: Aaron Copland, a seminal figure in Ojai Festival history.

in the air about public support for the arts. The ground breaking for New York City's Lincoln Center took place in 1959, accompanied by Aaron Copland's *Fanfare for the Common Man.*

Some of the newer composers were experimenting with the twelve-tone or serial technique of composition which abandoned traditional harmony and tonality. Most music lovers found these sounds to be incomprehensible and dissonant. Lawrence Morton recognized the need to build programs on the basis of box office attraction as well as to cultivate a market for pieces with little commercial appeal. As he said, "There's a lot of music going on that I don't happen to like; but I don't have to like it, I just have to see that it gets performed if it's representative of anything that is important in the world of music."

As early as 1949 Bauer was willing to put on new

music even though, as Morton observed that year, audiences were still "divided" in their reaction to "problematical" works. In his first program at Ojai as artistic director in 1954, Morton did introduce controversial new works. It was at that program that the format was changed to resemble the current one: five or six concerts performed over a shorter span of three days. That concentrated the audience and held the budget down. Also, it required a smaller number of players. Whereas Bauer had left programming up to the conductor, Morton took over this function himself, working closely with Robert Craft. Record crowds came to hear this "rare" music at the new Festival Bowl in the Civic Center Park. By Ojai's twenty-fifth anniversary in 1971, Morton would write, "The range of Ojai's interest is from the Middle Ages to tomorrow."

As for Ojai and his own years there, Morton said in 1966, "Well, I had it for seven years and then I was away from it since 1959, and I go back to it for the 1967 Festival. I don't know if I'll be glad about it or not because it is a very difficult job." He viewed Ingolf Dahl's "stint" there in a similar light: "I think three years is about as much as anyone can take of that. It is very, very hard work and very demanding." Morton also noted that Ojai was barely surviving on private funds with no city support: "They have the same kinds of problems that Monday Evening Concerts have. You have to go around and beg money from people."

The years 1954 through 1958 brought to Ojai for the first time Igor Stravinsky and Aaron Copland in pro-

Center: The banner in downtown Ojai proclaims an uncharacteristic direction for the Festival in 1960. Below: Henri Temianka who led the 1960 Festival.

grams which were among the most important the Festivals hosted. It was the first time Aaron Copland had ever conducted an orchestra. There was wide disagreement among critics about these first programs. While *L.A. Times* critic Albert Goldberg had his doubts, he liked the spirit of the programming and several of the performances.

As F. B. Vanderhoef, longtime Festivals watcher and friend of Lawrence Morton, remarked recently: "I can remember when *Sacre du Printemps* was the pits. Now it seems tame and lovely. We get educated. Lawrence Morton forced upon us a certain amount of adventurous stuff. And today Stravinsky seems old-fashioned after all these years of listening."

Leonard Stein, the pianist and musicologist, remembers: "It was inevitable that Stravinsky would conduct at Ojai and it was my good fortune to be able to perform *Les Noces* under his baton in 1956 ... [There was] the difficulty of coordinating the final repeated chords of the piece between the four pianos and the percussion. After several tries when the instruments failed to come together, he decided to omit the final two entrances, explaining that

> Lawrence Morton recognized the need to build programs on the basis of box office attraction as well as to cultivate a market for pieces with little commercial appeal.

the first performance of the work was held in a hall with a decided echo, about which we had no such concern here. Of course, only the composer himself could dare to make such a change in his music!" That program went out over the CBS radio network, the first time Festival concerts were broadcast nationally. The largest audience in Ojai history cheered. More tickets were sold for this entire series than ever before in the history of the Festivals; and so Morton was vindicated in his persistence in bringing these programs before the public.

After all this, a conflicted Festivals board canceled Morton for the following season while he was in Europe on a Guggenheim Fellowship. "People in Ojai had to hear something with a tune, or else they wouldn't buy the tickets," one Board member remarked in a 1983 interview. Morton was to return as artistic director in 1967. For some 30 years he advised the conductors, musicians and patrons who financed the Festivals. Looking back, his is a towering influence, but after his abrupt departure, 1960 became known as the year Ojai went "pop." Henri Temianka conducted singers Anna Maria Alberghetti, Dorothy Kirsten and John Raitt.

Top: Mezzo-soprano Grace Bumbry sings Copland's "Old American Songs" at Festival '58. Above: Soprano Dorothy Kirsten (1960). Top right: Robert Craft conducts at Festival '59. Far Right: A young Michael Tilson Thomas with composer/conductor Ingolf Dahl in the 1960s.

By popular demand, or at least the wishes of the Board, Lukas Foss returned in 1961 and stayed for the next three years. Under Foss's influence, the Festivals did not abandon its mission. In 1962, the young black virtuoso jazz flutist Eric Dolphy was invited to perform *Density 21.5* for solo flute by Edgard Varèse, as well as jazz and third-stream works. He also played saxophone that Festival and he was equally deft on bass clarinet. As a minority musician, Dolphy's appearance at a classical festival located outside of a major city was unusual, at a time when the Civil Rights drive of the 1960s was just getting underway. Lynford Stewart, who served as Festivals Treasurer for almost twenty years, recalls that after the Festival, Dolphy didn't have enough money to get to his next gig — a performance with John Coltrane in San Francisco. He hitched a ride. Dolphy died in Europe two years later at the age of 36.

By the 1963 Festival, Foss had redefined the goal of Ojai which had temporarily gone off track in 1960. He told Raymond Kendall of the *Los Angeles Times*, "...this is no mere concert series. The setting, the community, a 17-year-old tradition; all these make the Ojai Festival unique and dear to me... each program must satisfy in terms of musical enjoyment as well as intellectual curiosity."

By now local critics were calling the Festival "one of the most unusual of its kind anywhere." Certainly the opening program in 1963 supported that view. Foss led off with the experiment of performing music from *Don*

Giovanni with three orchestras, creating a kind of stereophonic surround-sound in the Bowl, not to everyone's delight.

Foss then slipped into Mozart's crowd-pleasing *Symphonie Concertante* with Eudice Shapiro on the violin along with her friend and colleague Sanford Schonbach on viola. Critics hailed this duo as "masterful," "impeccable," "luscious" and "technically perfect," while they described other performances that same evening as "cacophonies" designed to "irk lovers of music." Schonbach's one visit to Ojai was surely a footnote to his

> By Ojai's twenty-fifth anniversary in 1971, Morton would write, "The range of Ojai's interest is from the Middle Ages to tomorrow."

illustrious career as solo violist with the Los Angeles Philharmonic and Hollywood Bowl and his teaching career at the University of Southern California.

In 1964, a new home for the L.A. Philharmonic, the Music Center on Bunker Hill, opened its doors. Named for its chief benefactor, Dorothy Chandler, the new pavilion was seen as a forward-looking cultural development for the City of Los Angeles. In spite of the proximity and influence of this major addition to classical music venues, the Ojai Festival continued its independent course. The following year, President Lyndon Johnson and Congress created the National Endowment for the Arts, and the National Council on the Arts was formed with Isaac Stern as its chief musical representative. This new development promised an infusion of seed money into many localities. During the 1960s, union orchestras began to demand scale for rehearsal time, which became very expensive. This became a sticking point with the NEA, which balked at financing such time in their grants. But Ojai remained popular with musicians since ample rehearsal time was nearly always written into the budget.

In 1966, for Ojai's twentieth anniversary, David Raksin, the film music composer and a close friend of Lawrence Morton, wrote five special fanfares to be played throughout the concerts, conducted that year by Ingolf Dahl. Although Raksin is best known as the man who wrote the theme for the movie *Laura* (Raksin calls the

theme a "crossover" piece) he was always involved with so-called "highbrow" music, working closely with Morton at Monday Evening Concerts. Raksin dedicated one of the Ojai fanfares to Morton, and another to Copland. He recalled recently,

"The fanfares were written for brass because Dahl wanted them that way. I conducted the players. We hid behind the foliage. And they played it like demons... That music has gone on to become a famous fanfare — the main title of a [telecast] on Olympics' history, played by the Canadian Brass." Another "first" for Ojai.

Composer Frederick Lesemann, who served at Ojai during the Ingolf Dahl years (1964-1966) as musical director, manager and assistant conductor, recently recalled, "Ojai was a real watershed for me. The Festivals introduced me to musicians involved with new music. They were a multi-threat; the conductors, the performers, the breadth of musicianship. From the beginning Ojai was known. It has gone through changes over the years. Yet it hasn't lost its character and openness. Today, Ojai is known everywhere."

~ Ellen Malino James

Music Notes

John Henken

The 1957 and 1958 Festivals featured Aaron Copland, who was also the principal conductor. This was not a radical shift -- Copland's music had been heard before in Ojai and would be again. The Copland connection was another link in Morton's wide-ranging web of contacts, and Morton proved instrumental in persuading Copland onto the podium, not only for his own music but for a fairly broad repertory.

Above: Robert Craft, Eudice Shapiro and Ingolf Dahl, circa 1959. Left: Composer-in-Residence Luciano Berio (Festival '62). Below: Copland instructs soloists Sally Terri and Howard Chitjian during rehearsal of "The Tender Land" (1957).

By 1957 the afternoon orchestral concerts were being held in Ojai Civic Center Park, in what was called the Festival Bowl. For his first program, Copland included his Clarinet Concerto with Mitchell Lurie the soloist. Later that week he featured his *Twelve Poems of Emily Dickinson*, several of which were dedicated to artists/composers associated with Ojai. Copland's closer for 1957 was Act II and the finale of Act I from his opera *The Tender Land.*

For 1958 Copland conducted *Quiet City, A Lincoln Portait,* the first book of *Old American Songs,* with mezzo Grace Bumbry, and the West Coast premieres of his Orchestral Variations and Short Symphony (Symphony No. 2). He also led the world premiere of Leo Smit's Capriccio for String Orchestra and the West Coast premiere of Alexei Haieff's Piano Concerto, with Smit the soloist.

Robert Craft was again the principal conductor for the 1959 season, with premiere-free programming that represented fairly conservative retrenchment by Ojai standards. The influence of restive forces on the Ojai Board of Directors could clearly be seen. Other artists at the Festival that year were the Henri Temianka-led Paganini Quartet, pianist Natasha Litvin who gave a solo recital, the Gregg Smith Singers, and poet Stephen Spender, who presented a luncheon address entitled "Music as Poetry without

Words."

Lawrence Morton, his influence no longer in ascendance, had parted ways with the Board of Directors and remained absent for seven years. If 1959 was conservative, it was nonetheless substantial and thoroughly classical in perspective. The 1960 season, however, took a conspicuously pops direction. Temianka was the principal conductor that spring and the soloists included artists such as Anna Maria Alberghetti and the Alberghetti Family, John Raitt, and dancers Lotte Goslar and Company. When he came to record the Festivals' history for the 25th season (and updated it ten years later), Morton couldn't bring himself to list the repertory for 1960. None is given, in an otherwise scrupulously accurate survey.

Predictably, the pop experiment alienated many of the old Ojai supporters and failed to win new ones. For the next three seasons, artistic recovery fell to the mercurial Lukas Foss as music director/conductor/composer/pianist, with clarinetist Richard Dufallo listed as Festivals coordinator.

At first, 1961 looked much like 1959, with Foss leading a Baroque program featuring the Roger Wagner Chorale. Contemporary music seemed relegated to a Saturday morning chamber music program which included Carter's String Quartet No. 2 from the Peter Marsh-led Lenox Quartet and Leon Kirchner's Trio with violinist Eudice Shapiro, cellist Victor Gottlieb, and the composer at the piano. The finale, however, brought the Wagner Chorale and vocal soloists back for an agenda that included choral works by Webern, Schoenberg, and Hindemith, plus Stravinsky's *Pulcinella* and Foss' own *Introductions and Good-byes, A Nine-Minute Opera.*

The 1961 season also held a number of intriguing surprises, including an early post-modern spin with an improvisational concert featuring the trio of pianist André Previn, drummer Shelly Manne, and bassist Red Mitchell. The program ended with Previn and Foss improvising a four-hand encore at the piano. That spring the Festivals also provided scholarships to 20 young musicians, including

composers Edward Applebaum and Frederick Myrow, pianist/conductor Michael Zearott, bassoonist David Breidenthal, and oboist Barbara Winters, who were heard as performers and composers in informal programs. With stage lighting now installed, evening concerts as well as daytime events could be held in the Festival Bowl.

A four-day prelude of discussions and lectures/concerts with Luciano Berio, Milton Babbitt, Gunther Schuller, and Foss preceded the 1962 Festival proper. Ojai had a long tradition of informal Patrons' Concerts held prior to

the actual Festival, and this series took the concept public. The provocative mix reflected Foss's own interests, from quotation and recomposition (Berio) through serialism (Babbitt) to third stream and improvisation (Schuller).

The official weekend included a program of Mozart piano concertos with André Previn, Leo Smit, and Foss each taking turns at the keyboard and on the podium. It featured an evening of third-stream music from Schuller and the trio of flutist/saxophonist Eric Dolphy, bassist Jimmy Bonds, and drummer Milt Turner. There was also a morning of American choral music from the Roger Wagner Chorale, and a dramatic finale which featured the U.S. premiere of Stravinsky's *A Sermon, a Narrative, and a Prayer* and excerpts from Mozart's *Idomeneo.*

Lawrence Morton enjoyed the respect and admiration of many musicians, including Michael Tilson Thomas, above.

Ingolf Dahl, principal conductor during the mid-1960s, with violinist Eudice Shapiro.

In 1963, Foss took the Ojai adventure every which way. The opening concert mixed Mozart (always a favorite in Ojai, where taste generally favored the 18th and 20th centuries, skipping the Romantic middle of the orchestral repertory) with the U.S. premiere of Mauricio Kagel's polyglot *Anagrama,* the composer conducting. Then came the now customary chamber music program, followed by an evening which mixed an intriguing puppet show version of *Histoire du soldat* with classical Chinese music from pipa-master Lui Tsun-Yuen, singer/dancer Lui Hung, and the UCLA Chinese Performance Group. Sunday morning brought a slate of renaissance vocal music, and the finale was a large-scale performance of Bach's *St. John Passion.*

For the last three years of this Festivals decade, Ojai became a northern outpost of the University of Southern California. Lawrence Morton remained absent, but the directorship was entrusted to one of his closest friends, the respected Ojai and Monday Evening Concerts veteran and USC faculty composer, Ingolf Dahl. Frederick Lesemann was the Festivals' production manager, and many soloists/ensembles had close ties to the University of Southern California, including even the Trojan

String Quartet. Not surprisingly, this team produced programming quite congruent with the spirit of Lawrence Morton.

Dahl's opening program for 1964 featured Bach's D-minor Violin Concerto, with soloist Eudice Shapiro, and a concert performance of Mozart's *Zaide.* There was a choral program again, this time from the Berkeley Chamber Singers, and a program of avant-garde, mostly electronic music which introduced works by Babbitt, Conlon Nancarrow, Mel Powell, and Aurelio de la Vega, among others. On the Saturday evening orchestral concert Lillian Steuber played Schoenberg's Piano Concerto, while at the center of the genuinely quirky finale were Bruckner's Mass in E Minor and Dahl's own Concerto for Saxophone and Wind Orchestra.

The wind-band emphasis carried over into the next season, as Dahl launched the 1965 Festival with Mozart's C-minor Serenade, Ibert's Concerto for Cello and Wind Orchestra (Laurence Lesser, the soloist), and Colin McPhee's Concerto for Two Pianos and Wind Octet. Karl Kohn led a concert of medieval music, while the Saturday afternoon exploration of pioneering American music featured the Paul Shure-led Los Angeles String Quartet and a young pianist named Michael Tilson Thomas. For the Saturday evening capstone, Dahl shifted the ensemble emphasis to strings, giving the premieres of Harold Shapero's Serenade in D for String Orchestra and Ramiro Cortes' Concerto for Violin and Strings (the soloist Eudice Shapiro), followed by Handel's *Dixit Dominus,* with singers Delcina Stevenson, Nina Henson, and the USC Concert Choir.

Dahl closed his leadership tenure in 1966 with a Festival featuring flutist Doriot Anthony Dwyer in two programs from the Boston Symphony Chamber Players and as soloist Saturday evening in Bach's B-minor Overture and Nielsen's Flute Concerto. The earlier Saturday events were a Baroque program with Eudice Shapiro and the William Hall Chorale, and a chamber concert of experimental music running from 15th-century polyphony to the West Coast premiere of *Echoi* by Lukas Foss. This 20th Festival was also decorated with fanfares specially composed for the Festival by film great David Raksin, another friend of Lawrence Morton.

HISTORY OF THE OJAI FESTIVAL BOWL
known popularly as the Libbey Bowl

From 1947 to 1951, most of the Festival concerts were held in Nordhoff (now Matilija) auditorium, seating 400. Other venues were the Art Center Theater, the Community and Presbyterian churches, the Ventura Junior College auditorium and private residences.

1952 First outdoor concerts (2) in the park.

1953 Two concerts in the park. During the concerts on Ojai's main street adjoining the park, stores were closed and traffic was blocked.

1954 One concert in the park. A temporary stage was built in the park bowl, designed by Roy C. Wilson of Santa Paula and Austen Pierpont of Ojai.

1955 Permanent seats were added in the Bowl.

1956 Permanent benches were installed, doubling seating capacity. The Bowl stage was repaired and remodeled with new canvas roof.

1957 A shell was erected over the stage, designed by Austen Pierpont and Roy C. Wilson. This replaced the annual canvas cover, two of which had been destroyed by fire or vandalism. A stage storage room was also built. The Bowl seating capacity was now 750 plus lawn.

1958 A Civic Center Bowl Committee was formed to act as a clearing house for use of the Bowl and to take charge of maintenance.

1959 New lighting permitted the first night-time outdoor performance in Festival history.

1960 For the first time, all five concerts were held in the Festival Bowl in Civic Center Park.

1961 Flaring torches and costumed ushers at the evening concerts.

1962 Free cider was served during intermission at the Friday night concert plus singing on the lawn by the Gregg Smith Singers.

1966 Improvements to the Bowl stage: "eyebrow" on the upper rim; acoustical baffles around the rear wall; radiant heating in the floor.

1967 The old Tennis House was removed from the Bowl to make room for about 260 new seats in the Terrace, increasing total capacity to just under 1,000 plus lawn seating.

1973 The Bowl in Libbey Park (formerly Civic Center Park) was officially named the Ojai Festival Bowl. It was built in 1954 and improvements added in 1965-67.

1974 First-time use of a stage extension, to accommodate the large Philharmonic Orchestra. Carpet strips were used to pad the seats in the center audience section.

1980 The Rotary Club took on the project of building dressing rooms for the Bowl, which were completed in time for the Festival. These were much appreciated by the performers, who previously had had no place to wash their hands or store their instruments.

Part 3

REFLECTING THE TIMES

*"When I think of Ojai I think of the faces, voices, and music of so many friends...
it is not just the artists or the planners who make a festival great. The sponsors,
patrons, and audience of this Festival are extraordinary. It is quite incomprehensible
for people who have never visited Ojai to comprehend how rustic, sophisticated,
and friendly a place it is. As I think back on my early days at the Festival,
I remember also great friends among the audience like Connie Wash, Patsy Eaton
Norris, Louise Rousseau, Beatrice and Bob Cunningham..."*

~ Michael Tilson Thomas

THE CONDUCTORS

1967	Pierre Boulez
1968	Robert LaMarchina, Lawrence Foster, Michael Tilson Thomas
1969	Michael Zearott, Stefan Minde, Michael Tilson Thomas, Lalo Schifrin
1970	Pierre Boulez
1971	Gerhard Samuel
1972	Michael Zearott, Richard Lert
1973	Michael Tilson Thomas
1974	Michael Tilson Thomas
1975	Michael Tilson Thomas
1976	Aaron Copland, Sidney Harth, William Kraft

1967 marked the return of Lawrence Morton as artistic director. The Festival, then in its twenty-first year, welcomed Pierre Boulez in his fifth American appearance. In homage to a composer among the pioneers of twentieth-century sound, Boulez included works by Edgard Varèse.

On Sunday morning Boulez shared the conductor's podium with a youthful Michael Tilson Thomas, who conducted Mozart's Serenade in E-flat, for Wind Octet after intermission. This program represented the more traditional music which Festival goers had come to expect on Sunday mornings. And yet, as old-timers remember it, Karlheinz Stockhausen's *Zeitmasse* came as a jarring shock to many listeners this bucolic Sunday morning. Lawrence Morton called Stockhausen's 1956 work "enormously important to contemporary music."

The actor Jeff Corey, who served on the Festivals Board, would later perform as reader of Stravinsky's *Oedipus Rex*. Corey also worked with Lawrence Morton. "He was a rock formation. He had an independent mind," Corey recalls. "Morton would patiently go through brochures of who was available and what their price was. He had a plan of going to the Board with the question of who do you like and who would you consider. It was refreshing... People who kept the thing going were not people sophisticated in music."

Ralph Grierson, verstile keyboard soloist, Hollywood studio musician and composer, has performed frequently at the Festivals. He reminisced in a recent interview about Ojai: "I grew up with the Festivals. At USC, I had studied with Dahl. My first Ojai was in 1967 with Boulez, one of the most brilliant musicians I knew. I had

been married a year. We stayed with townspeople and made friendships. The townspeople knew that this was important work and they tried very hard to like it."

Fred Hall agrees with that assessment of the support Ojai gave the Festivals in those years. A former President of the Festivals, Hall recalls working closely with the Rotary Club to finally raise enough money to build dressing rooms for the artists during the late 1970s. For three decades prominent conductors had been "camping out." In 1955, Stravinsky used a tent; during the 1960s, Foss took a nap on plastic trash bags behind the stage; and in 1976 Copland walked up the road to Fred and Gita Hall's house and asked to use the facilities.

Left: Patsy Eaton Norris, a key supporter and former President of the Festivals. Above: The San Francisco Dance Spectrum in 1971. Below right: Gerhard Samuel, who conducted Festival '71.

Hall, an expert on jazz, organized with Lynford Stewart a series of jazz events for Sunday mornings at the Festivals, which eventually spun off into a separate "Jazz at Ojai" festival of its own. The proceeds from their annual jazz events were donated to the Festivals.

As Festivals President, Hall worked closely with Connie Wash's daughter, Patsy Eaton Norris, who herself would later serve as Festivals President. Whereas previous board members were "locals" only, Hall, then Eaton Norris, expanded the membership of the Board to include a wider circle from outside of Ojai.

The 1968 program brought Stravinsky's memorial to Aldous Huxley, five or six minutes of Variations composed in 1963-64 which Lawrence Morton said might be "tough going" for some of the audience. Sunday morning the LaSalle Quartet had as guest pianist young James Levine, who was later to become conductor of the Metropolitan Opera.

The following day longtime Festival watchers braced themselves for the second coming of Stockhausen, in the first American performance of the final version of *Punkte*, (Points) written between 1954 and 1966. Morton remarked that Tilson Thomas "studied it intensely for this performance (and has stubbornly refused to loan me my own score!)"

The work of Michael Hennagen was included in a 1969 program that highlighted repertoire for multiple choirs. Those were years of protest against the "establishment" and the Vietnam War, and Hennagen used a text by folk singer Pete Seeger. There was also *This Is the Word* by Greenwich Village composer j. marks, which borrowed from rock and electronics with a text by the 1930s social protest folk singer Woody Guthrie. *Election 1968*, by Gregg Smith and two members of his chorus, recreated the

sounds of the political conventions. That was also the year of the Chicago Seven's defiant protest at the Democratic convention.

The year 1970 brought the return of Pierre Boulez, by now a familiar presence in Ojai. The program included the first American performance of his *Domaines* for solo clarinet and six instrumental groups. It was also the first year that the Los Angeles Philharmonic appeared in Ojai. Throughout the decade (in 1971, 1974, 1976 and 1978), the Philharmonic would return to play at the Festivals, as it does to this day.

1971 marked the debut of Gerhard Samuel as conductor and artistic director. This was the first and only time that a Festival was almost rained out. Samuel worked with the staff to relocate the concert indoors and to change the program to fit a smaller space. Miraculously, the skies cleared just in time for the opening program.

In 1972, Michael Zearott returned to conduct the Ojai Festival Orchestra in Gunther Schuller's Symphony for Brass and Percussion. Schuller was known to Ojai audiences for his *Variants on a Theme of Thelonius Monk*, performed in a 1962 concert, and as the composer who was just then rediscovering "ragtime" music and bringing about its revival. Scott Joplin's rags and waltzes would be

Above: Boulez conducts in 1967. Festival '72 had a strong multi-cultural theme, including a Balinese Gamelan (right) and a West African drumming group (bottom). Bottom far right: Will Geer, who narrated in 1976.

featured in a program during the 1974 concerts.

A decidedly ethnic flavor came with the 1972 Festival under the baton of Michael Zearott. He included a program of popular music of the Mariachi from Jalisco, Mexico; drum music from West Africa; and the Balinese Gamelan Angklung. A consciousness of other cultures was just being recognized during these years; and some members of the audience came dressed in ethnic-inspired fashions of the day.

In 1976 Aaron Copland returned to conduct. Political issues continued to have an impact on programs in the aftermath of the Vietnam War. Composer William Kraft recalls that his composition *Des Imagistes*, for reader and percussion sextet, generated a minor controversy. Narrator Will Geer refused to read a passage he considered pro war. Geer's daughter, Ellen, read it instead, and Geer later read an anti-war statement of his own.

Betty Izant is the current box office manager and archivist of the Festivals, and for many years was the chief administrator of the Festivals' office. Perhaps her credo can best describe what the Festivals meant in those years of activism and social protest:

"I believe in music and the arts. They are what remain of a civilization after the wars have been forgotten. The Ojai Festival is a small but important source of spiritual food in a disordered world."

~ Ellen Malino James

Music Notes

John Henken

The start of the Festivals' third decade represented a real watershed. On the first page of the 1967 program booklet was the declaration, "S. Hurok Presents Pierre Boulez." However unlikely the pairing of culture's master salesman and music's establishment-twitting arch rebel might have seemed, the results for Ojai were definitive.

1967 also marked the second appearance of Lawrence Morton as artistic director. The vita given as Boulez' biography in the program booklet proudly — and justifiably — listed the composer's U.S. career

to date solely in terms of his appearances on Morton's Monday Evening Concerts series. In the event, Boulez proved to be a sure and satisfying program builder, something he was given little credit for at the time in conventional circles. The fascinating opening program began — after a now-legendary delay to allow an 'orange' train to pass — with Schoenberg's String Quartet No. 2 (Grace-Lynne Martin, the soprano) in the composer's string orchestra arrangement, continued with Debussy's *Danses* (with harpist Dorothy Remsen), and finished with Bartók's Music for Strings, Percussion, and Celeste.

Boulez' other ensemble programs nicely balanced relative adventure with progressive familiarity, as when he opened the Saturday evening agenda with four Varèse classics and closed it with Stravinsky's *Les Noces*. Sunday morning he led a performance of Stockhausen's *Zeitmesse,* to which Michael Tilson Thomas responded

Left: Lawrence Morton introduced Pierre Boulez to Ojai in 1967. Above: Festival '68 featured the LaSalle String Quartet. Near left: James Levine, who was a piano soloist in 1968.

with Mozart's E-flat Serenade. For the Festival finale Boulez scheduled his *Éclat* with Tilson Thomas the piano soloist, but he followed it with Schubert's "other" C-major Symphony, No. 6. This care even extended to the Saturday morning chamber program, which pianist Easley Blackwood began with his own *Fantasies* and Boulez' fierce Second Sonata and ended with the lyric graces of Schumann's *Dichterliebe* (accompanying baritone Elwood Peterson).

After that experience came two seasons of conducting troikas. For 1968 the Debut Orchestra of the Young Musicians Foundation (with Ingolf Dahl as music

Far left: Boulez during his first Ojai appearance in 1967. Near left: Johanna Kirkland and John Clifford of the Los Angeles Ballet. Below: Aaron Copland continued to occupy an important place in Ojai's affections, appearing again in 1976.

director) was in residence, led by Robert LaMarchina, Lawrence Foster and Michael Tilson Thomas. From the ground-breaking LaSalle Quartet came two chamber music programs featuring the string quartets of Witold Lutoslawski and Earle Brown, and Schumann's Piano Quintet with James Levine, among other works.

For 1969 the orchestra was again Ojai's own, led by the trio of Tilson Thomas, Michael Zearott, and Stefan Minde, and Stravinsky was the tie that bound. Zearott's program offered Stravinsky's last published works, his instrumentation of two songs by Hugo Wolff as well as the world premiere of Lalo Schifrin's *Variants on a Madrigal of Gesualdo* with the composer conducting. Minde's agenda began with *Apollon Musagète*, and Tilson Thomas closed the Festivals with *Canticum Sacrum* and the Bach Chorale and Variations arrangement which had had its premiere at the Ojai Festival back in 1956.

Pierre Boulez returned to Ojai in 1970, this time with nothing less than the Los Angeles Philharmonic, with which he was beginning a close and enduring association. The opening program, however — Stravinsky, Stockhausen, and the U.S. premiere of Boulez' own *Domaines*, with Mitchell Lurie the clarinet soloist — was per-

formed by the Ojai Festival Orchestra. The winds of the Philharmonic contributed to the all-Berg Saturday matinee, while the strings were on call for the evening, when Boulez' *Livre pour cordes*, promised for 1967 (ready for the moment, but to be revised again), was finally heard in Ojai. Following a program of morning ragas from sitarist Nikhil Banerjee (with Kanai Dutta, tabla), Boulez and the Philharmonic closed with a program of completely characteristic breadth: Schoenberg's Chamber Symphony No. 1, Mahler's *Songs of a Wayfarer* (Timothy Nolen, baritone), Webern's Opus 30 Variations and Opus 6 Six Pieces, and Stravinsky's *Firebird* Suite in the 1919 orchestration.

For the expansive 25th anniversary Festival in 1971, Gerhard Samuel was artistic director and conductor, although Morton again provided the program annotations and a valuable survey of Festival artists and repertory. "Prelude Evenings" of pantomime and a Chinese shadow play with music by Lou Harrison,

William Colvig, and Richard Dee prefaced the Festival. Also included were "A Celebration to the Sun" offered in three performances by the San Francisco Dance Spectrum, and a postlude in the form of three environmental compositions by Morton Subotnick. This programming reflected the times — Ojai was always ahead of the counter- and multicultural curve — and it also made a fitting anniversary reminder of the Festivals' early interest in theater of all kinds.

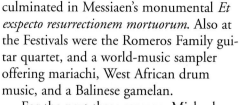

Samuel opened with the Ojai Festival Chamber Orchestra, and Bach and Berio. The progressive music director of the Oakland Symphony for 12 years, Samuel was finishing his first season as associate conductor of the Los Angeles Philharmonic and he had that ensemble at his disposal for the Saturday evening and Sunday afternoon concerts. Between those two concerts Lou Harrison's Chinese Classical Music Ensemble presented a morning survey of Chinese music. Samuel's orchestral programs featured the first performances of Charles Boone's *Chinese Texts* and Yuji Takahashi's *Kagahi* with the composer as the piano soloist. There was also Mozart's C-minor Mass with the Pomona College Glee Clubs and Piano Concerto in E-flat, K. 271 (Takahashi again the soloist), Schumann's "Rhenish" Symphony No. 3, and Stravinsky's Concerto in D for String Orchestra.

In 1972 Michael Zearott returned, to a less ambitious Festival. Budget-busting years followed by leaner, more concentrated seasons, had become a familiar Ojai cycle. Most imposing that spring was the Saturday evening program for woodwinds, brass, and percussion, which

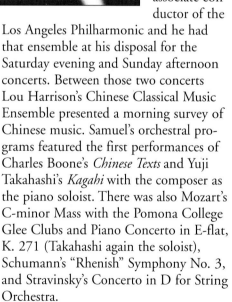

Top: Michael Zearott conducted at Festival '72. Above: Ojai was an important element in the developing career of Michael Tilson Thomas, music director in 1973, '74 and '75.

culminated in Messiaen's monumental *Et exspecto resurrectionem mortuorum*. Also at the Festivals were the Romeros Family guitar quartet, and a world-music sampler offering mariachi, West African drum music, and a Balinese gamelan.

For the next three seasons, Michael Tilson Thomas was at the artistic helm of the Festivals. Already a veteran of Ojai Festivals — as well as the Boston Symphony, the Buffalo Philharmonic, and the New York Philharmonic's Young People's Concerts — the young conductor had come early to Lawrence Morton and Monday Evening Concerts. The programming revealed the influence of Morton as clearly as it did Tilson Thomas' own interests.

Highlights of this Tilson Thomas tenure included a 1973 program of music for multiple keyboards which brought minimalism to the Festivals with Steve Reich's *Four Organs with Percussion*, plus John Cage's *Three Dances for Two Amplified Prepared Pianos*, both in their West Coast premieres. Also presented was an homage to five Ojai composer/conductors (also 1973) featuring the world premieres of Lukas Foss' *Orpheus*, Ingolf Dahl's *A Noiseless, Patient Spider*, and Aaron Copland's *Threnodies I and II*, with Boulez' *Éclat/Multiples* and Stravinsky's *Symphony of Psalms*. Tilson Thomas' tenure also saw the inauguration of annual jazz concerts; and the world premiere of Charles Wuorinen's *A Reliquary for Igor Stravinsky* (1975), a joint Ojai Festival/Buffalo Philharmonic commission.

1976 brought Copland back to the Festivals, this time with the Los Angeles Philharmonic, and returned Lawrence Morton to the staff list as artistic advisor. The featured ensemble for the Friday opening, however, was the Los Angeles Ballet, in a mixed bill of Balanchine and John Clifford. Saturday evening Copland conducted his own *Statements*, *Inscape*, and Piano Concerto, with Lorin Hollander the soloist, and Mendelssohn's "Italian" Symphony No. 4 to close. For the Festivals finale, Copland chose Mahler's Fourth Symphony (Polly Jo Baker, soprano) and his own rarely heard, bravura *Symphonic Ode*.

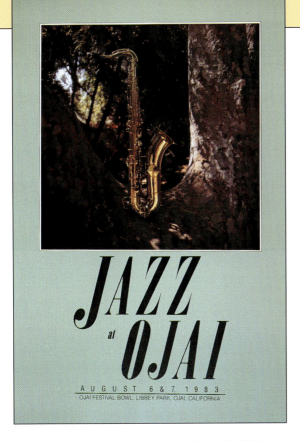

Festival '61 featured the jazz trio of André Previn, Shelly Manne and Red Mitchell, below.

JAZZ AT OJAI

Jazz, that very American genre, has had its place in the history of the Ojai Festival. It first appeared in 1961 with the André Previn, Shelly Manne, Red Mitchell Trio and in 1962 with the Eric Dolphy Trio. It reared its lively head again in 1973, and for a full decade the Sunday morning programs of the annual Festival were devoted to jazz.

In producing these events, Fred Hall and Lynford Stewart, experts in jazz, were later joined by Gene Lees, jazz authority and publisher of the monthly Jazz Letter. Eventually, the Sunday morning programs spun off into a separate festival of their own. For three years, beginning in 1981, a weekend in August offered lively listening to jazz aficionados. Some of the best-known groups and soloists came to perform in the festival known as Jazz at Ojai.

1961	The Previn - Manne - Mitchell Trio
1962	Eric Dolphy Trio
1973	Roger Kellaway Cello Quartet
1974	Ralph Grierson and the Southland Stingers
	Buell Neidlinger and the El Monte Art Ensemble
1975	Tom Scott and the L.A. Express
1976	Toshiko Akiyoshi and The Big Band, with Lew Tabackin
1977	Sonny Stitt Quintet
	The Catalyst All-Stars
	Oscar Peterson
1978	The Ray Pizzi Jazz Quartet
1979	The Akiyoshi/Tabackin Big Band
1980	The Heath Brothers
1981	The Ray Brown All Stars
1982	Bobby Hutcherson Quartet
	Bobby Shew Sextet

JAZZ AT OJAI - AUGUST

1981	The Benny Carter All Stars, John Best and Abe Most, Buellgrass
1982	Roger Kellaway Trio, Wild Bill Davison and his Wild Cats, Dick Cary and his Jazz Masters, Phil Woods Quartet, Jimmy Witherspoon and the Dirty Dozen
1983	Superband with Betty O'Hara, Gary Le Febvre Quintet, Bobby Shew Quintet, Subramaniam and Friends.

Robert LaMarchina conducted the twenty-second Festival in 1968 (left). Below: Daniel Lewis, music director in 1981 and 1983.

THE ARCHIVES
PART 3 & 4

TWENTY-FIRST FESTIVAL
May 19-21, 1967
Conductor: Pierre Boulez
Assistant Conductor: Michael Tilson Thomas
Artistic Director: Lawrence Morton
Performers: Ojai Festival Orchestra
   Ojai Festival Wind Ensemble
   Pomona College Glee Clubs
   Easley Blackwood - composer/pianist
   Lloyd Bunnell - bass
   Larry Jarvis - tenor
   Christina Krooskos - contralto
   Grace-Lynne Martin - soprano
   Dorothy Remsen - harp
   Michael Tilson Thomas - piano
   Genevieve Weide - soprano

TWENTY-SECOND FESTIVAL
May 24-26, 1968
Conductors: Robert LaMarchina, Lawrence Foster,
Michael Tilson Thomas
Artistic Director: Lawrence Morton
Performers: The Debut Orchestra of the
   Young Musicians Foundation
   LaSalle String Quartet
   Kathleen Lenski - violin
   James Levine - piano
   Judith Raskin - soprano
   Karl Ulrich Schnabel - piano

TWENTY-THIRD FESTIVAL
May 23-25, 1969
Conductors: Michael Zearott, Stefan Minde, Michael Tilson
Thomas, Gregg Smith, Lalo Schifrin (guest conductor/composer)
Artistic Director: Lawrence Morton
Performers: Ojai Festival Orchestra
   The Gregg Smith Singers
   Hayden Blanchard - tenor
   Peter Hewitt - piano
   Christina Krooskos - mezzo-soprano
   Milton and Peggy Salkind - piano four-hands
   Paul Shure - violin
   Sheridon Stokes - flute

TWENTY-FOURTH FESTIVAL
June 5 - 7, 1970
Conductor: Pierre Boulez
Artistic Director: Lawrence Morton
Performers: Los Angeles Philharmonic Orchestra
   Ojai Festival Chamber Orchestra
   Nikhil Banerjee - sitar
   Hayden Blanchard - tenor
   Rafael Druian - violin
   Kanai Dutta -tabla
   Michael Gallup - bass
   Robert Hasty - baritone
   Larry Jarvis - tenor
   Mitchell Lurie - clarinet
   Karl Kohn - piano
   Timothy Nolen - baritone
   Jayne Proppe - mezzo-soprano

TWENTY-FIFTH FESTIVAL
May 26 - 30, 1971
Conductor: Gerhard Samuel
Assistant Conductor: Phillip Lehrman
Administrator: Stanley Weinstein
Performers: Ojai Festival Chamber Ensemble
Los Angeles Philharmonic   Ralph Grierson - piano
Les Masques Blancs   Peter Mark - viola
Lou Harrison and Friends   Timothy Nolen - baritone
Pomona College Glee Clubs   Kenneth Rexroth - poet
Red Gate Players   Elise Ross - soprano
San Francisco Dance Spectrum   Morton Subotnick - electronics
Lorene Adams - soprano   Yuji Takahashi - piano
Patricia Brooks - soprano

TWENTY-SIXTH FESTIVAL
May 26-28, 1972
Conductor: Michael Zearott
Guest Conductor: Dr. Richard Lert
Performers: Ojai Festival Orchestra
   Los Angeles Chamber Orchestra
   Roger Wagner Chorale
   Balinese Gamelan Angklung
   The Mariachi UCLATAN
   The Romeros
   I Madé Bandem - dancer
   Kwasi Badu - Ashanti drummer
   Michael Zearott - piano

TWENTY-SEVENTH FESTIVAL
June 1-3, 1973
Conductor: Michael Tilson Thomas
Administrative Director: Richard F. Perry
Performers: Ojai Festival Orchestra
   Glendale Symphony Orchestra
   The Pacifica Singers
   Pomona College Glee Clubs
   Roger Kellaway Cello Quartet
   Jesse Levine - viola
   Lukas Foss - piano
   Ralph Grierson - piano
   Craig Hundley - piano
   Roger Kellaway - piano
   Michael Tilson Thomas - piano

TWENTY-EIGHTH FESTIVAL
May 31, June 1-2, 1974
Conductor: Michael Tilson Thomas
Artistic Coordinator: Frederick Lesemann
Performers: Ojai Festival Chamber Ensemble
   Ojai Festival Childrens Chorus
   Los Angeles Philharmonic
   The El Monte Art Ensemble
   The Southland Stingers
   UCLA A Capella Choir
   David Evitts - baritone
   Gilbert Kalish - piano

Michael Wager - actor
Paul Zukofsky - violin

TWENTY-NINTH FESTIVAL
May 30 & 31, June 1, 1975
Conductor: Michael Tilson Thomas
Artistic Coordinator: Heidi Lesemann
Performers: Ojai Festival Orchestra
California Boys' Choir
USC Concert Choir
Arriaga Quartet
Los Angeles Brass Quintet
Tom Scott & the L.A. Express
Buswell - violin
Claudine Carlson - mezzo-soprano
Ralph Grierson - piano
Su Harmon - soprano
Michael Tilson Thomas - piano

THIRTIETH FESTIVAL
May 21-23, 1976
Conductor: Aaron Copland
Artistic Director: Lawrence Morton
Performers: Los Angeles Philharmonic
Los Angeles Ballet
Toshiko Akiyoshi Big Band
Polly Jo Baker - soprano
Will Geer, Ellen Geer - readers
Lorin Hollander - piano

THIRTY-FIRST FESTIVAL
June 3-5, 1977
Conductor: Michael Tilson Thomas
Artistic Coordinator: Heidi Lesemann
Performers: Ojai Festival Chamber Orchestra
California Boys' Choir
Ventura County Master Chorale
Ralph Grierson - piano
Red Holloway - tenor saxophone
Harvey Pittel - saxophone

THIRTY-SECOND FESTIVAL
May 19-21, 1978
Conductor: Calvin Simmons
Artistic Coordinator: Heidi Lesemann
Performers: Ojai Festival Chamber Orchestra
Los Angeles Philharmonic
Pomona College Choir
African Music and Dance Ensemble (Cal Arts)
The Ray Pizzi Jazz Quartet
Edward Auer - piano
Jonathan Mack - tenor

THIRTY-THIRD FESTIVAL
May 18-20, 1979
Conductor: Lukas Foss
Artistic Director: William Malloch
Performers: Ojai Festival Chamber Orchestra
Irvine Master Chorale
Akiyoshi/Tabackin Big Band
The Firesign Theatre
Ralph Grierson - piano
Werner Klemperer - narrator
Ravi Shankar - sitar

THIRTY-FOURTH FESTIVAL
May 23-25, 1980
Conductor: Lukas Foss
Artistic Director: William Malloch
Performers: Ojai Festival Chamber Orchestra
Days Months & Years To Come Ensemble
The Heath Brothers
Los Angeles Ballet
Sequoia String Quartet
Sonor

Ventura County Master Chorale
Marvin Hayes - bass-baritone
Jonathan Mack - tenor
Mary Rawcliffe - soprano

THIRTY-FIFTH FESTIVAL
May 29-31, 1981
Conductor: Daniel Lewis
Artistic Director: William Malloch
Performers: Ojai Festival Chamber Orchestra
Irvine Master Chorale
Mladi Wind Quintet
Sequoia String Quartet
Marvin Hayes - speaker
Jonathan Mack - tenor
Peter Nagy - piano

THIRTY-SIXTH FESTIVAL
June 4-6, 1982 Stravinsky Centennial
Conductor: Robert Craft
Artistic Director: Lawrence Morton
Performers: Ojai Festival Chamber Orchestra
Pacific Chorale
Bobby Shew Sextet
Marvellee Cariaga - mezzo-soprano
Jeff Corey - narrator
Paul Jacobs and Gilbert Kalish - duo-pianists
Douglas Lawrence - baritone

THIRTY-SEVENTH FESTIVAL
June 3-5, 1983
Conductor: Daniel Lewis
Artistic Director: William Malloch
Performers: Ojai Festival Orchestra
Kronos Quartet
The Musicians of Swanne Alley
Brenda Boozer - mezzo-soprano
Swapan Chaudhury - tabla
Ravi Shankar - sitar

THIRTY EIGHTH FESTIVAL
June 1-3, 1984
Conductor: Pierre Boulez
Artistic Director: Lawrence Morton
Performers: Los Angeles Philharmonic
AMAN Folk Ensemble
New Wave Chamber Players
Claudine Carlson - mezzo-soprano
Charles Rosen - piano

THIRTY-NINTH FESTIVAL
May 31, June 1 & 2, 1985
Conductor: Kent Nagano
Composer-in-Residence: Olivier Messiaen
Artistic Director: Jeanette O'Connor
Performers: Los Angeles Chamber Orchestra
The Women of the Pacific Chorale
Tokyo String Quartet
Jeanne Loriod - onde Martinot
Yvonne Loriod - piano
Lucy Shelton - soprano

FORTIETH FESTIVAL
May 30 & 31, June 1, 1986
Conductors: Kent Nagano, Stephen Mosko
Artistic Director Emeritus: Lawrence Morton
Artistic Coordinator: Jeanette O'Connor
Performers: Los Angeles Philharmonic
Kronos Quartet
E.A.R. Unit
Pacific Chorale
Jamee Ard - mezzo-soprano
Susan Narucki - soprano
Ursula Oppens - piano
Dorothy Stone - flute

45

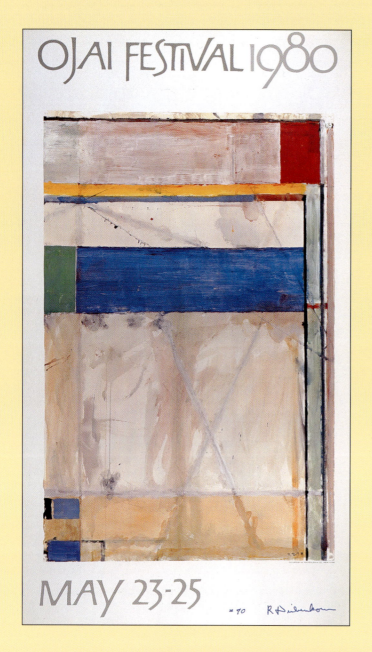

OJAI FESTIVAL 1980

MAY 23-25

#90 R Diebenkorn

OJAI FESTIVAL 1982

JUNE 4-6

Ojai Festivals commissioned a series of artists' posters, mainly during the 1980s, by artists such as Diebenkorn, Motherwell, Hockney, Goodnough and Noland (clockwise from top left).

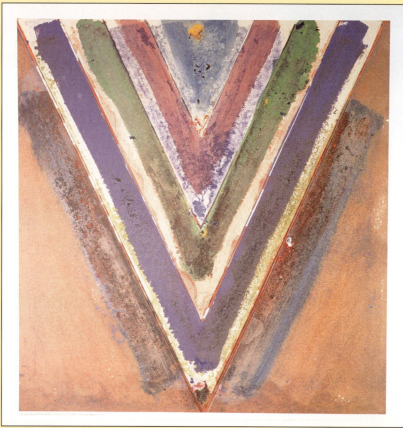

OJAI FESTIVAL 1986

MAY 30-JUNE 1

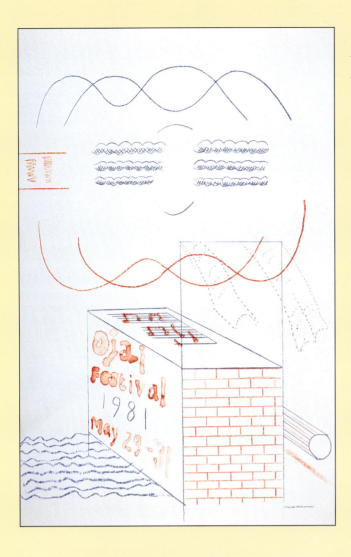

OJAI FESTIVAL
MAY 31–JUNE 2 1985

Part 4

CONSOLIDATION

"Certainly it is Ojai's unique blend of musical and natural beauty that powers its ability to inspire and refresh. Each season Ojai brings to the table new works that advance the cultural palate that much further, and can there be any question that this kind of growth is vital to the very nature of every art? In this sense the Ojai Festival can be said to be very much a state of mind, and how musicians and listeners alike approach the music and allow it to affect them is uniquely at the core of this event's success for fifty years."

~ Jeanette O'Connor
Festivals Administrator

THE CONDUCTORS

1977	Michael Tilson Thomas
1978	Calvin Simmons
1979	Lukas Foss
1980	Lukas Foss
1981	Daniel Lewis
1982	Robert Craft
1983	Daniel Lewis
1984	Pierre Boulez
1985	Kent Nagano
1986	Kent Nagano, Stephen Mosko

It was a beautiful place to make music, as Lukas Foss recalled recently about his years in Ojai. "We had the courage to take a chance and make people sit up and take notice... Nowadays conductors are supposed to be good fundraisers," he remarked. Foss's long association with the Festivals spans several decades. He first came in 1953 to play his virtuoso piano, then again to conduct the 1961, 1962 and 1963 seasons, returning in 1979, 1980 and 1987.

Did Ojai change from the sixties to the eighties? "No," Foss replied. "It was always forward-looking. My repertoire was always American composers," Foss said, even though he was European educated. He came to this country when he was fifteen years old and remem-

cians, she recalls, were "like thoroughbred race horses eager to get out of the gate."

"Morton was the premier impresario of our time," said O'Connor, who worked closely with him during her tenure at the Festivals. "He raised the form of programming to an art. We tried to keep it as subtle as possible, combining pieces with one another. They were intertwined. On paper, Bach and Berg might seem like a weird combination. But with the ears the music makes sense."

With Bill Malloch, O'Connor said, "The money wasn't there and he still made the Festivals an artistic success." *Los Angeles Times* music critic Martin Bernheimer aptly described Malloch as "composer, broadcaster, critic, teacher, disc jockey, musicologist, iconoclast, author and eccentric."

Malloch was especially proud of the 1979 concert which featured film music to be performed alongside the films themselves. Music by George Antheil (*The Jazz Symphony* and *Ballet Mécanique*) and scores by Arnold Schoenberg, Darius Milhaud and Erik Satie played while

Above: Lukas Foss's association began in 1953 and continued through the late 1980s. Right: Composer William Malloch was an important influence as the Festival's principal administrator during the early 1980s.

scenes from the films, Murnau's *Nosferatu*, Charlie Chaplin's *The Adventurer*, René Clair's *Entr'acte Cinematographique*, and Fernand Léger's and Dudley Murphy's *Ballet Mécanique* played across a big screen set up in the Libbey Bowl. Satie's music, as Malloch points out, was the only score written expressly for the René Clair film with which it played. Silent films, accompanied by continuous music, were, says Malloch, a "new way for musicians to make an honest living... So major composers gradually became involved... All the films and music on that program reflected the early 1920s, that burst of experimentation and energy."

O'Connor recalls rehearsing the music for *Nosferatu*: "There was no track to go by, so [the conductor Lukas] Foss had to use his skill to pull it off, to pace it. He had to watch the screen as he would watch an opera for cues from the actors. As the music built to a huge crescendo, and then a pause, the hero in the film ducked under the covers. The audience laughed at this confluence of music and visuals coming together. It was a very popular program."

Malloch also brought Ravi Shankar to Ojai for the first time that year. The Indian sitar virtuoso who had performed with Beatle George Harrison at the 1971 Concert for Bangladesh, came with his East Indian ensemble. They attracted record crowds, who trekked to Ojai in spite of the gasoline crisis that year. Ravi Shankar returned in 1983.

Mrs. George French Porter, whose home long served as a haven for conductors and musicians, hosted Ravi Shankar on his second visit to Ojai. She had an authentic

bers that "Copland was the turning point." At Ojai, there was always enough rehearsal time, he said. "That was generous. But I didn't hold out for a specific fee. I liked the place so I did something for less. And I never forced my music on the organization." He didn't have to. The Festivals played a half dozen of his compositions starting in 1953 through the 1980 program that he conducted.

Jeanette O'Connor remembers Foss well when she was working at the Hollywood Bowl while studying conducting and composition in 1976. "Unlike other conductors, Foss was always approachable." Through Foss, O'Connor met William Malloch who served during those years as artistic director of the Festivals. She signed on as his assistant, and during the 1980s became the full-time administrator of the Festivals.

O'Connor recalled that Foss always knew intuitively how much time a rehearsal would take. And with Lawrence Morton that system was further enhanced. "Morton had a way of figuring it out and scheduling it in advance," she recalled. "Could you run over a particular session? What about the brass, the percussion?" The musi-

Indian breakfast prepared. Shankar and his troupe called her from the guest house: "Where are the corn flakes?"

The 1980 program included *The Art of Fuguing*, Malloch's orchestrations for Bach's *The Art of the Fugue*. Malloch noted: "In my orchestral appreciation of Bach's work, I have tried to let light in upon the subject... It is meant to amuse as well as instruct." Foss later recorded this piece, and it has remained popular.

In 1984 Pierre Boulez returned to a sold-out Ojai Festival. Since his last visit to Ojai in 1970, his career had taken him to New York, where he led the Philharmonic through seven seasons, and then to Paris to direct IRCAM (Institut de Recherche et de Coordination Acoustique/Musique) and the Ensemble InterContemporain. There he explored electronic and computer music, expanding the range and sound of musical instruments. Following the performance of *Éclat/Multiples*, at Festival '84, the string players from the Los Angeles Philharmonic who had performed the demanding piece surprised the maestro by wearing T-shirts emblazoned with the words "I survived L'Éclat!"

In 1985, conductor Kent Nagano made his Ojai debut after winning the Seaver Conductor's Award. He later worked with Pierre Boulez. "Boulez was kind, generous," said Nagano. "He invited me to attend his classes. He presented me with the collected editions of the poetry of Stéfane Mallarmé and he suggested I read them. His approach was not one-dimensional but multi-dimensional. He is one of the great musicians of our time."

At the 1985 Festival which Nagano conducted, Fred Lamb, who has long served on the Festivals' Music Committee, saw Nagano as "delightful and vibrant." "A festival in particular should present something new, not the regular standard fare. It is amazing to expand one's understanding and learn to like things that seemed quite difficult at first. Bartók's Third Quartet is a good example. The first time I heard it, I thought it was a bunch of noise. Now it seems purely melodic. We must continue to give the opportunity to have these works heard."

~ Ellen Malino James

Top: Ravi Shankar appeared at the 1979 and 1983 Festivals. Left: Conductor Kent Nagano returned to Ojai many times. Below left: Nagano with soprano Jamee Ard in 1986.

Music Notes

John Henken

The fourth decade of the Festivals was a period of concentration and consolidation of Ojai traditions and ideals. This could be seen in the artists and, most conspicuously, in the repertory. All-Bach and all-Mozart programs distinguished many Festivals, but there were also composer-specific Festivals, such as the Stravinsky centennial in 1982 or the Messiaen-centered Festival in 1986.

At the same time it was a period of transition. Or rather, one of transmission, passing on the traditions and ideals as well as the challenges and the rigorous

sense of self-criticism to new musicians, some of whom had grown up with the Ojai Festivals.

An example of this was Michael Tilson Thomas. He returned to lead the 1977 Festival, opening with a Bach program. His Saturday evening program featured a provocative mix of sacred and secular music, including Berio's *Chemins II B/C* and Messiaen's *Trois petites liturgies de la Présence Divine.* The closing concert matched Ruggles' and Ives' stalwart Americana with Tchaikovsky's "Little Russian" Symphony No. 2. The now-traditional chamber concert Saturday afternoon was distinguished by the world premiere of Morton Subotnick's *Liquid Strata,* his second composition involving "ghost" electronics.

Succeeding Tilson Thomas at Ojai in 1978, as he did with the New York Philharmonic's Young People's Concerts on CBS, was the young black conductor Calvin Simmons. At that time Simmons was the assistant conductor of the Los Angeles Philharmonic, and that ensemble was again in residence for the Festival. Simmons began with an Ojai rarity, an evening of Hispanic music. The program included seldom-heard works by Carlos Chávez, Heitor Villa-Lobos, and Claudio Santoro, as well as Falla's *El Retablo de Maese Pedro* in a staged performance. He turned to another pillar of 20th-century musical drama, Igor Stravinsky, for the climax of the Saturday evening concert, *Oedipus Rex*, with a cast that included Jerold Norman in the title role and Marvellee Cariaga as Jocasta. The 1978 Ojai Festival was one of the many bright achievements of a tragically short career, which ended when Simmons drowned at the age of 32.

For the next two seasons Lukas Foss was the music director and the artistic director was the equally multi-hyphenated William Malloch, broadcaster-author-composer-critic. The 1979 Festival was launched by a striking evening of music by Schoenberg, Milhaud, Satie and Antheil, accompanying silent films. The Festival also included one of Ravi Shankar's Eastern fusion programs and a rare performance of the Hindemith/Brecht *Lehrstück,* involving audience-participation and a cast that included the Firesign Theatre and Werner Klemperer as the narrator.

Both the 1979 and the 1980 Festivals demonstrated Malloch's interest in Bach. The imposing roster of

visiting ensembles to the 1980 event list-ed the Sequoia Quartet, the UC San Diego-based SONOR, the Los Angeles Ballet, and the Canadian new music group Days, Months, and Years to Come.

In 1981 and again in 1983 the music director was Daniel Lewis, the beloved director of the USC Symphony then coming to the end of his distinguished tenure as conductor of the Pasadena Symphony. (Malloch was again artistic director for those years.) Highlights of Lewis' first Festival were performances of Lou Harrison's striking Mass, Carlos Chávez' Symphony No. 5, the West Coast premiere of Benjamin Britten's *Our Hunting Fathers* (with tenor Jonathan Mack), and the U.S. premiere of Clementi's Symphony No. 4. In 1983 Ravi Shankar returned. The Kronos Quartet and The Musicians of Swanne Alley made their Ojai debuts. Lewis' orchestral repertory included Milhaud's Symphonic Suite No. 2 (Protée) and Martinu's Concerto for Two String Orchestras, Piano, and Timpani. KUSC, Los Angeles, recorded the concerts for rebroadcast on American Public Radio.

In between the Lewis years came the Stravinsky centennial in 1982, entrusted once again to Robert Craft, with the very hands-on help of Lawrence Morton. With the exception of the Sunday morn-ing jazz concert, each of the programs featured the music of Stravinsky with other works that had inspired him in some fashion. Ojai had shown its admi-ration for Stravinsky often, presenting all or part of nearly 40 compositions by the master.

For 1984, Pierre Boulez was again the musical director, hard on the heels of the important Festival Boulez/LA organized by the Los Angeles Philharmonic and with that orchestra again in residence. Opening night, however, belonged to AMAN, the wide-ranging folk ensemble. Charles Rosen offered a demanding solo piano recital consisting of Stravinsky's Serenade in A, Boulez' Sonata No. 3, and Beethoven's "Diabelli" Variations. The orchestral works included Boulez' work-in-progress *Éclat/Multiples* (which had already visited Ojai in an earlier incarna-tion), Schoenberg's Chamber Symphony No. 1, and Webern's Opus 21 Symphony.

The 1985 Festival featured the music of Olivier Messiaen, master of Christian mysticism and birdsong, and a formative influence on Boulez. For the music directorship Boulez recommended the brilliant young American conductor Kent Nagano, whom Boulez had recently appointed as chief guest conductor of the Ensemble InterContemporain in Paris. With Messiaen attending, the Festival began with a piano recital by his wife Yvonne Loriod. The Tokyo String Quartet had in hand the Saturday chamber concert, and the orchestra for the

Stephen "Lucky" Mosko conducted the Saturday evening concert in 1986 (left). Below: The Kronos Quartet, appearing in 1986. Below left: Kent Nagano with orchestra and soprano Susan Narucki in 1986.

Angeles Philharmonic. It was composer-conductor-percussionist Stephen Mosko, however, on the podium for the first orchestral concert, Saturday evening. His program featured the West Coast premiere of John Adams' *The Chairman Dances,* the "foxtrot for orchestra" inspired by his work on *Nixon in China,* plus Mozart's "Haffner" Symphony No. 35 and Stravinsky's Symphony in C. For the closing concert Nagano led *Messages of the late R.V. Troussova* (with soprano Susan Narucki) by György Kurtág, Schoenberg's Chamber Symphony No. 2, and Beethoven's Fantasia in C minor for Piano (Ursula Oppens), Chorus (the Pacific Chorale), and Orchestra.

More of Kurtág's tiny, precise imagery was on display in the opening concert, a typically heady brew from the Kronos Quartet. Nagano conducted works in the Saturday matinee, an equally venturesome voyage with the California E.A.R. Unit. During the Messiaen year the traditional Sunday morning jazz concert had given way to a song recital (soprano Lucy Shelton with pianist Lambert Orkis) and that pattern continued in 1986 with a solo recital from Ursula Oppens, which

weekend was the Los Angeles Chamber Orchestra. Saturday evening Nagano conducted Messiaen's vast tribute to Utah rock formations, *Des canyons aux étoiles* and closed the Festival with Messiaen's *Trois petites liturgies de la Présence Divine.*

With the success of the Messiaen venture, Nagano was invited back the following season, this time with the Los

also included a Kurtág set of pieces, *Splinters.*

The generational shift that occurred during Ojai's fourth decade left the Festival well-positioned for its fifth. Seven of those ten years would be guided by conductors from that decade. Much of the enduring success of the Festival can be attributed to just this sort of organic growth — evolution rather than revolution.

Part 5

KEEPING THE SPIRIT ALIVE

"Looking back over Ojai history, the Festivals has a history of giving people a chance before they become really recognized for their talents. Stravinsky, Boulez, Tilson Thomas. It is an important pivotal point for a lot of artists... And there is the unusual mingling with people. Real people. The absence of slickness. No pretense. No feigning or pretending. That is refreshing... How well-defined and distinct its artistic mission is... Great guiding lights like Lawrence Morton moved the Festivals toward presenting the future of music... People don't struggle with this in Ojai. It will be around for another fifty years. Pureness of mission has given it a tradition that is old by California standards."

~ Kent Nagano

THE CONDUCTORS

1987	Lukas Foss
1988	Nicholas McGegan, Peter Maxwell Davies, Diane Wittry
1989	Pierre Boulez
1990	Stephen Mosko
1991	John Harbison, Peter Maxwell Davies
1992	Pierre Boulez
1993	John Adams
1994	Michael Tilson Thomas
1995	Kent Nagano
1996	Pierre Boulez

Dazzling soloist Mari Kodama (1995).

Pierre Boulez as Leonard Bernstein's successor at the New York Philharmonic rejected the standard repertoire. "Let's have a laboratory," he said. "Why be afraid of flouting tradition?" For the Philharmonic's 150th anniversary in 1993, Boulez said that he preferred controversial music to a "slow death."

Certainly nothing was more controversial than the 1990 Ojai Festival. Stephen "Lucky" Mosko, leading light of the new American music, took over the post of music director and Elliott Carter settled in as composer-in-residence. For the first time in the Festivals' history, no music from the past was on the program nor any by European composers.

Mosko, who was born the same year the Festivals began (1947), called his season's offerings "Recent Views from America." "This is music," he said, "that a generation of listeners raised on rock and roll can really relate to — music that is intellectually challenging, yet enormously rewarding both emotionally and visually." Mosko called this music "all-American...of our own time and our own century." But the swing of the pendulum had reached its limit for Ojai audiences, and the following year brought more harmonious fare under the direction of John Harbison and Peter Maxwell Davies.

Boulez returned in 1992 with the Los Angeles Philharmonic and a new collaborator, innovative Peter Sellars, who staged Stravinsky's *Histoire du soldat* in its fifth incarnation at Ojai. The first had taken place in a memorable performance during the 1948 season; another (with puppets) in 1963, and again in 1985 and 1988.

Sellars, who was then directing the Los Angeles Festival, was also creative consultant to the Los Angeles Philharmonic. He had directed hundreds of theatrical productions and several important new operas, including John Adams' *Nixon in China* and *The Death of Klinghoffer*. From the Kennedy Center to Glyndebourne and American and British television, Sellars approached each new production with a fresh, up-to-the-minute interpretation. For instance, he changed the setting of

The Marriage of Figaro to New York's Trump Tower.

No one was particularly surprised when Sellars announced he would be including inner-city actors in the cast of *A Soldier's Tale* for opening night at Ojai. That spring, South Central Los Angeles had experienced the worst riots of its history in the wake of the Rodney King verdict. Sellars, ever conscious of the moment, staged the production from the back of a flatbed pickup truck with

an all-black cast. The performance featured two female rappers named T-Love and Suggah B as narrators, who put their own spin on C. F. Ramuz' original libretto.

Stravinsky's soldier became a jeans-clad youth; the Devil, a street hustler and the scenery changers wore army fatigues. Sellars had transformed a now traditional Ojai piece into a post-riot commentary on capitalism and militarism.

John Adams, who had collaborated with Sellars on both his operas, took the Ojai podium in 1993 to conduct a weekend of twentieth century music. The Festival included works by John Cage, Steve Reich and Henryk Gorecki. Jazzy pieces by Ravel and Copland, and Adams' rousing *Grand Pianola Music* added zest to the "popular culture" theme of these concerts.

For a still youthful Michael Tilson Thomas, the 1994 Festival was a poignant journey back to his roots in Ojai. The pieces he chose, especially those by his former mentor Ingolf Dahl, and compositions by Ojai conductors Copland, Stravinsky and Foss, reflected his nostalgia for those earlier Ojai Festivals where he had literally grown up as music director during four of the seasons in the 1970s.

Like Tilson Thomas, Kent Nagano returned to Ojai. Before the 1995 Festival, Nagano said: "Coming back to Ojai is one of the big occasions in my career. Ojai gave me a chance when I was relatively unknown... I owe the Festivals a lot." Regarding Ojai's influence in music circles, Nagano states, "It is influential directly and indirectly. Leaf through the names involved as participants or soloists or as music directors. It is an impressive list of people well known in performing circles — known for innovation and development and evolution of music. Copland, Stravinsky, Boulez [are] towering figures in the history of music, and they were the founding building blocks of what the Ojai Festival has become."

What about the people who say they don't understand twentieth century music? Nagano sees this attitude as "usually a request for help, assistance in understanding the music... extra time, extra effort or care... to develop a passion for music." Nagano, who conducted Boulez'

Mémoriale in 1995 said, "It shattered people's negative impressions. Beauty is a form of communication. That piece communicates things that are meaningful today. Take the time, the patience..."

Ara Guzelimian, artistic director of the Festivals, said in a KUSC interview just before the 1995 Festival: "We've tried to explain Ojai to members of the Lyon Orchestra, who have never been here, what the atmosphere is like. We've said, 'It's just a small town park with a band shell and big trees and old wooden benches and it retains a kind of relaxed, rustic sensibility'... The Festival is still a kind of homey, family operation. You don't send your artist liaison department and a limo to the airport. I go pick them up holding a sign and a French flag. Joan Kemper was at the Bowl this morning supervising the new paint job. It's a very hands-on operation."

Joan Kemper came into the Festivals under the wing of Patsy Eaton Norris. "Patsy was responsible for my involvement," Kemper said. "The organization was in the red. There was talk of closing the Festivals. Patsy intro-

Above: Current Artistic Director Ara Guzelimian Left: Nagano leads the Lyon Opera Orchestra in Milhaud's "Le boeuf sur le toit" (1995).

duced me to long-time supporters who were quite angry with the administration, so in the beginning I was repairing broken bridges. Patsy never asked anyone to do anything for the Festivals that she wouldn't do herself."

During the 1996 Festival, Kemper hopes to inaugurate OSCAR, the Ojai Summer Camp & Arts Retreat, a two-week residential arts experience for disadvantaged teenagers, to be held at Thacher School. "I would like this to be the jewel in the fiftieth anniversary crown," Kemper said. "In the Festivals tradition of encouraging and inspiring future artists, this camp will open doors for underserved youth, helping them turn creative potential into artistic ability. These young people will see that there are viable options in life that involve the arts. Perhaps well-known artists will come to teach here. Big names. Who knows? Maybe Boulez..."

Pierre Boulez returns to Ojai in 1996 with the Los Angeles Philharmonic and the pianist Mitsuko Uchida as principal soloist. Boulez will conduct members of the Los Angeles Philharmonic in three concerts. One will be devoted entirely to his own work. As of this writing, other featured composers will include Ravel, and Stravinsky. Mitsuko Uchida will be playing both with the

> *"What interests, attracts, even fascinates me as a performer is the incandescence of great works, which can always be rekindled."*
>
> ~ Pierre Boulez

orchestra and in recital.

"This year is Boulez' seventieth birthday and he's been celebrated everywhere," said Ara Guzelimian. "The Ojai Music Festival discovered Boulez as early as the 1960s. He was music director in 1967 before he was known except to that happy band at the Monday Evening Concerts."

In the current debate over private patronage and government support, the ultimate question is how to sustain artistic excellence in a democratic society. There is always a tension between popular tastes and the artists' standards of excellence. And, in a highly graphic, sometimes amusing way, Ojai demonstrates that tastes in music are, in the end, highly subjective. Music is, after all, one of the most emotional of the arts.

In Ojai a hard lesson was always understood from the beginning: that the artistic success of a concert or a musical composition is not decided by consumers but by those who create the art. Whether or not audiences liked the work of innovators such as Edgard Varèse, a pioneering master of twentieth century music, other composers realized his importance early on. The formative influences came as much or more from each other as from public recognition.

Left: Nicholas McGegan, conductor, and Malcolm McDowell, narrator in Purcell's "King Arthur" (1988). Right: Nicholas McGegan, music director of Festival '88. Below: Pierre Boulez, who returns in 1996. Below right: The Kronos Quartet provided an exciting opening to Festival '93.

Ideally, artists are supposed to lead the culture, not follow it. Musical tastes are decided by the artists themselves, not the impresarios, the audience, or the donors. But musicians and composers have always had to contend with the age-old struggle between commerce and art. This was the ground from which John Bauer created the first Festival in 1947 when he negotiated with the Los Angeles impresario L.E. Behymer over the fee for Ojai's first performing artist, baritone Martial Singher.

T
he mission of Ojai today is to continue what it started out to do a half century ago: to present new or unfamiliar music and to educate current audiences as well as future generations.

John and Helen Bauer, who began the Festivals and guided the programs during the first seven years, and Lawrence Morton, who took over in 1954 and remained involved "on and off" for the next thirty years, had different philosophies and styles. Yet they shared a desire to make a mark for themselves as champions of new music.

For all of them, Ojai became the vehicle. And, in strikingly different ways, they all loved the Valley. Morton's sister, Beatrice Cunningham, often stayed in Ojai. The Bauers, after moving to San Francisco, made frequent visits to their Ojai home. John Bauer and Lawrence Morton died within a decade of one another; Bauer in 1978, Morton in 1987. Bauer's ashes are buried at two different sites on his former property in the East End of Ojai, and Morton's are scattered somewhere in the Ojai Valley as

well — evidence of the sentimental feeling Morton had for Ojai.

During the first fifty years of the Festivals, the music has ranged from the traditional to the avant garde, and experimentation has flourished. Innovative artists from all over the world have come, bringing their gifts. Here at Ojai, they were allowed the artistic freedom to stretch creative bounds, supported by a friendly, unpretentious yet sophisticated community. Since 1947, each Festival has been challenged to nurture the public's affection for the event while holding fast to the progressive edge of twentieth century music.

~ Ellen Malino James

Music Notes

John Henken

During its fourth decade, the Ojai Festivals had begun a trend toward composer-specific or thematic Festivals. This continued in its fifth decade, with the idea formalized to the point of having composers-in-residence, such as Elliott Carter and Peter Maxwell Davies.

Of course, many Festivals had featured a particular composer's work — usually because that composer was also on the podium. Ojai has been very supportive of conducting composers, beginning with Stravinsky and Copland. The former came to the Festivals with an established history as a conductor (of his own works), but Lawrence Morton was always proud of the formative role the Festivals played in bringing Copland to the podium.

Holding an important place among Ojai's composer-conductors is Lukas Foss, who returned in 1987 for his sixth season over a period spanning more than half of the Festivals' life. The 1987 Festival featured works by Foss, but in a broader

Top: Conductor Lukas Foss, returning in 1987 for his sixth season. Above: Pierre Boulez continues to be a huge influence, returning for the sixth time in 1996. Bottom right: Peter Maxwell Davies was composer-in-residence for Festival '88, returning in 1991.

context of neo-Renaissance or neo-Baroque compositions matched with period originals. This was most appropriate for a Festival honoring the memory of Lawrence Morton, who had died earlier that year. Foss had brought a portion of Charles Wourinen's *The Magic Art, an Instrumental Masque after Purcell* to Ojai in 1980 — this time Foss prefaced Wourinen with actual Purcell. The same program offered the first West Coast performances of Oliver Knussen's *Music for a Puppet Court* and Foss's own *Renaissance Concerto* (with flutist Carol Wincenc).

Not surprisingly, the 1987 Festival offered a generous supply of Bach, Handel, and Vivaldi, as well as the work of modern nostalgists such as David Del Tredici and outright arrangements of ear-

lier material, such as Copland's *Old American Songs*. The Pacific Chorale, under John Alexander, sang a clever program of Medieval and Renaissance music with modern variations and reinterpretations interspersed, including the world premiere of Daniel Kessner's *Alea-luia* and the West Coast premiere of Foss's *De Profundis*. Foss closed with the U.S. premiere of Joan La Barbara's *Helga's Lied* and the West Coast premieres of John Harbison's *The Flight into Egypt* and his own Percussion Concerto.

The final program of 1987 had begun with the *Four Tallis Voluntaries* by Peter Maxwell Davies, a composer long fascinated with his musical antecedents. The following year Maxwell Davies was composer-in-residence at the Festivals, which had an English emphasis, in part because the first UK/LA Festival had so assiduously promoted British arts. The 1988 Festival also had a title, "Fanciful Legends," as did each of the individual programs. The much-prized Baroque opera specialist Nicholas McGegan was the music director that year and his

splendid period band, the Philharmonia Baroque Orchestra, was also in residence.

McGegan opened with Purcell's "semi-opera" *King Arthur,* with a cast that included Malcolm McDowell narrating. Saturday morning saw a performance of Davies' pantomime opera

Cinderella, with a cast of Ventura County children. In the afternoon the California E.A.R. Unit offered more Davies and that hardy Ojai perennial, Stravinsky's *L'Histoire du soldat*. For the evening, Davies took the podium of the Ojai Festival Chamber Orchestra for Beethoven's "Eroica" Symphony and the U.S. premieres of his own *Into the Labyrinth* (Neil Mackie, tenor) and *An Orkney Wedding, with Sunrise* (the chamber orchestra version). The Festival ended with a concert featuring the U.S. premiere of Davies' Oboe Concerto, with Stephen Colburn the soloist, and the counter-typecast McGegan at the head of *Petrushka*.

In 1989 the featured composer was György Ligeti, the Transylvanian master of sonority and micro-polyphony, although there was also a strong minor in Stravinsky. And since the music director was Pierre Boulez, Festival-goers also had ample opportunity to catch up on the current state of his meditations. When Boulez first came to Ojai, he was virtually unknown as a conductor, and feared in many circles as an uncompromising composer and fierce polemicist. By the 1980s Boulez had become one of the world's most esteemed conductors, the austere "French correction" to the Bernstein years at the New York Philharmonic. That he continued to return after Morton's death testifies to the depth of his feeling for Ojai, a place where he found a commitment and an idealism to rival his own.

Boulez opened the 1989 Festival with a program of choral and solo song, featuring Ligeti's *Lux aeterna* and climaxing in Stravinsky's *Les Noces*. The Los Angeles Philharmonic was again the orchestra of record, and for his first orchestral program, Boulez scheduled Ligeti's *Apparitions* (West Coast premiere) and Double Concerto (with flutist Janet Ferguson and oboist David Weiss), plus Stravinsky's *Le Rossignol*, with a strong cast headed by Phyllis Bryn-Julson in the title role.

The finale was all-Boulez: *Livre pour cordes; Éclat; Mémoriale* (Anne Diener Giles, flute); and *Trois improvisations sur Mallarmé*, with Bryn-Julson. Boulez is famous for the years — decades — in which he allowed his music to develop in concept and technique. The Arditti Quartet provided a rare opportunity to hear his early *Livre pour quatuor*, which evolved into *Livre pour cordes*, a piece which has only recently reached a state its composer regards as finished.

Stephen "Lucky" Mosko was the music director for 1990 and Elliott Carter — with the descriptor "Dean of American composers" now inevitably attached — was the composer-in-residence. This season a California Institute of the Arts connection was as apparent as the USC ties were in the Dahl years. Minimalism and performance art provided provocative contrast to the music of Carter, which had first stirred Ojai as early as 1953 when the Walden Quartet stunned Festival-goers with the West Coast premiere of his First String Quartet. The California E.A.R. Unit offered an afternoon devoted to Carter's chamber music, while Ole Bühn was the protagonist in Carter's Violin Concerto in a performance a month after Bühn had delivered the premiere in San Francisco. On Sunday programs, Mosko led his San Francisco Contemporary Music Players and soprano Susan Narucki in Carter's *A Mirror on Which to Dwell* and the Ojai Festival Chamber Orchestra in *Penthode*.

The Mozart bicentennial cast its long shadow

John Harbison (top) and Peter Maxwell Davies shared the directorship of the 1991 Festival.

over the 1991 Festival. The Ojai experience of the Mozart year proved reflective and discriminating. Composer-conductors John Harbison and Peter Maxwell Davies shared the music directorship and the conducting duties, and the Festival programs listed just those three composers: Harbison, Davies, and Mozart. The Scottish Chamber Orchestra was in residence, and produced its own soloists for the U.S. premieres of Davies' "Strathclyde" Concertos Nos. 3 and 4. Davies also introduced an Ojai Festival Overture.

Harbison placed an emphasis on somber, reflective vocal music, with his *Words from Paterson* sung by Sanford Sylvan and his *Elegiac Songs* sung by

Janice Felty. The Los Angeles Master Chorale sang the world premiere of Harbison's *Ave, Verum Corpus,* matched naturally with Mozart's sublime setting of the same text. Harbison also offered his *Exequien for Calvin Simmons,* an instrumental tribute to the former Ojai music director who died young.

Old friends were on hand for the Festivals in 1992, both on the stage and on the programs. Pierre Boulez was music director and the Los Angeles Philharmonic was the orchestra. The Philharmonic's New Music Group provided the ensembles opening night, for Schoenberg's *Pierrot Lunaire* (featuring Phyllis Bryn-Julson) and Stravinsky's *Histoire du soldat,* in a provocative new truck-bed staging by Peter Sellars reflecting post-riot anxieties. Ojai's signature piece, the venerable *Soldier's Tale* now matched three generations of iconoclasts — composer, conductor, director — who collectively have probably done more than anyone else to shape dramatic music in the 20th century. Stravinsky loomed large throughout the Festivals, which also honored the memory of the recently deceased Olivier Messiaen.

John Adams, his ensemble leadership abilities already proven as the creative chair of the St. Paul Chamber Orchestra's artistic triumvirate and on the podia of leading orchestras, was the latest in Ojai's long and honorable lineage of composer-conductors as the music director for 1993. His selection also confirmed Ojai's particular affection for composers noted for dramatic music such as opera, ballet and music theater. In that sense Adams and Maxwell Davies represented the latter years of Ojai's half-century as characteristically as Stravinsky and Copland did earlier decades.

Adams' joyful examination of vernacular influences featured the Kronos Quartet, the Los Angeles Philharmonic New Music Group, pianist Paul Crossley, and the Los Angeles Chamber Orchestra. John Cage, who had died less than a year before, was honored with performances of some of his most characteristic works, including *Indeterminacy* (read by Charles Shere) and a garland of songs and sonatas performed by Joan La Barbara and Gloria Cheng.

For his seventh Festival, Michael Tilson Thomas brought the training ensemble he founded, the New World

Below: John Adams presided at Festival '93. Michael Tilson Thomas (left) and Kent Nagano (above) continued to hold Ojai close to the heart, returning in 1994 and 1995 respectively.

Symphony, to Ojai in 1994. His wide-ranging programming brought together many threads of Ojai history, clearly reflecting the spirit of Lawrence Morton. Stravinsky, Copland, Dahl, and Foss were all represented by important works. In addition to his orchestra and ensembles made up of members of the orchestra (the Plymouth String Quartet, the New World Brass Quintet, and the SouthBeat Percussion Group), the artists included baritone Thomas Hampson, pianist Ralph Grierson, and flutist Paula Robison.

Kent Nagano returned to Ojai in 1995, for a lively focus on dramatic, narrative, and programmatic music, much of it with a French accent. Nagano's Lyon Opera Orchestra provided the Festival's pillars, between which a family performance by the West African Dance Ensemble Sona Sane and a sophisticated exploration of words and music from flutist Eugenia Zukerman and actress Claire Bloom could be enjoyed.

With the arrival of the Scottish Chamber Orchestra and the Lyon Opera Orchestra, the Ojai Festivals might seem to have entered, in a small way, the world of touring orchestras making the summer festival circuit. It is worth noting that both orchestras came not as complete strangers, under the leadership of previous Festival directors. The Festivals and its partisans have sometimes prided themselves on the label "the little Salzburg," an appellation that now seems a kind of oxymoron. If comparisons must be sought, chamber music-oriented Lockenhaus would be a better

match for the intimacy, idealism, and adventure of Ojai (which, of course, is not to suggest any influence — Ojai was up and running decades before Gidon Kremer launched his Austrian enterprise).

In truth, whatever the ambitions of some of its leaders, Ojai has always been a kind of counter-festival, where it was not bigger and more, but smarter and different that mattered. As a result, there are many festivals, particularly in California, which in their heart of hearts would be proud and flattered to be considered a "little Ojai," in spiritual descent if not actual size.

For the 50th season in 1996, Pierre Boulez and the Los Angeles Philharmonic return for fresh encounters with the music of Stravinsky and Boulez. For Ojai the creative path is a spiral — firmly rooted but always reaching out, constantly rediscovering its past while embracing the future.

THE ARCHIVES
PART 5

FORTY-FIRST FESTIVAL
May 29-31, 1987
Conductor: Lukas Foss
Artistic Director Emeritus: Lawrence Morton
Artistic Coordinator: Jeanette O'Connor
Performers: Ojai Festival Chamber Orchestra
    Pacific Singers
    David Del Tredici - piano
    Lukas Foss - piano
    Joan La Barbara - soprano
    Susan Narucki - soprano
    Carol Wincenc - flute

FORTY-SECOND FESTIVAL
June 3-5, 1988
Conductors: Nicholas McGegan, Peter Maxwell Davies,
Diane Wittry
Artistic and Executive Director: Jeanette O'Connor
Performers: Ojai Festival Chamber Orchestra
    Philharmonia Baroque Orchestra
    California E.A.R. Unit and Friends
    Nancy Armstrong - soprano
    Neil Mackie - tenor
    Malcolm McDowell - narrator

FORTY-THIRD FESTIVAL
June 2-4, 1989
Conductor: Pierre Boulez
Artistic and Executive Director: Jeanette O'Connor
Performers: Ojai Festival Chamber Orchestra
    Los Angeles Philharmonic
    Pacific Chorale
    Arditti String Quartet
    Phyllis Bryn-Julson - soprano
    Jonathan Mack - tenor
    Ursula Oppens & Alan Feinberg - duo piano
    Leonard Stein - piano

FORTY- FOURTH FESTIVAL
June 1-3, 1990
Conductor: Stephen Mosko
Composer-in-Residence: Elliott Carter
Artistic and Executive Director: Jeanette O'Connor
Performers: Ojai Festival Chamber Orchestra
    California E.A.R. Unit
    Cantinova
    San Francisco Contemporary Music Players
    Ole Böhn - violin
    Joan La Barbara - soprano
    Susan Narucki - soprano
    Rachel Rosenthal - performance artist
    Frederick Rzewski - composer and pianist

FORTY-FIFTH FESTIVAL
May 31, June 1 and 2, 1991
Conductor: John Harbison, Peter Maxwell Davies
Artistic Director: Christopher Hunt
Performers: Scottish Chamber Orchestra
    Los Angeles Master Chorale
    Janice Felty - mezzo-soprano
    Dennis James - glass armonica
    Sanford Sylvan - baritone

FORTY-SIXTH FESTIVAL
May 29-31, 1992
Conductor: Pierre Boulez
Artistic Director: Ara Guzelimian
Performers: Los Angeles Philharmonic
    Peter Sellars - Stage Director
    Phyllis Bryn-Julson - soprano
    Cho-Liang Lin - violin
    André-Michel Schub - piano

FORTY-SEVENTH FESTIVAL
June 4-6, 1993
Conductor: John Adams
Artistic Director: Ara Guzelimian
Performers: Los Angeles Philharmonic New Music Group
    Los Angeles Chamber Orchestra
    Kronos Quartet
    Gloria Cheng - piano
    Paul Crossley - piano
    Joan La Barbara - soprano

FORTY-EIGHTH FESTIVAL
June 3-5, 1994
Conductor: Michael Tilson Thomas
Artistic Director: Ara Guzelimian
Performers: New World Symphony Orchestra
    Ralph Grierson - piano
    Thomas Hampson - baritone
    Margaret Lattimore - mezzo-soprano
    Paula Robison - flute

FORTY-NINTH FESTIVAL
June 9-11, 1995
Conductor: Kent Nagano
Artistic Director: Ara Guzelimian
Performers: Lyon Opera Orchestra
    Miczka Quartet
    Claire Bloom - narrator
    Yukiko Kamei - violin
    Mari Kodama - piano
    Susan Narucki - soprano
    Angelina Réaux - soprano
    Sanford Sylvan - baritone
    Eugenia Zukerman - flutist

Bibliography

UNPUBLISHED SOURCES

Lawrence Morton, *"Monday Evening Concerts,"* typescript of an oral history interview conducted 1966 by Adelaide Tusler for the Oral History Program, Department of Special Collections, University Research Library, University of California, Los Angeles, 1973, 603 pages.

Lawrence Morton Papers, 1908-1987, Special Collection Number 1522, Department of Special Collections, University Research Library, University of California, Los Angeles.

Although the inventory does not mention Ojai in connection with the Aaron Copland section of these manuscripts, Morton's correspondence with the composer does refer to Copland's visit to the Festivals.

Lawrence Morton, "Stravinsky in Los Angeles." (Los Angeles: Los Angeles Philharmonic Association, 1982)

Ojai Festivals, collection of John and Helen Bauer. Office files and personal papers consisting of some 9,000 items, The Huntington Library, San Marino, California.

The Huntington Library also holds the papers of Los Angeles impresario L.E. Behymer with whom Bauer was associated for a brief time.

The Sol Babitz mss., not yet cataloged, can be found in the UCLA Music Library, Special Collections. Also in the Music Library:

Donald Christlieb, *"Remembrance of Lawrence Morton"* (n.d.)

Arthur and Herbert Morton, *"The Lawrence Morton Years: 1954-1971,"* (Lawrence Morton Foundation, 1993)

PUBLICATIONS

Babitz, Eve, *"Keeping Time in Ojai,"* Westways (June, 1995)

Boulez, Pierre, *Notes of an Apprenticeship* (New York: Knopf, 1968)

Boulez, Pierre, *Boulez on Music Today* (Cambridge, Massachuetts: Harvard University Press, 1971)

Bryan, Robert, *"In the Key of Ojai,"* Westways (May, 1976)

California's Musical Wealth: Music in California, overview summary (Southern California Chapter of Music Library Association, 1988)

Clark, Sedgwick, ed., *Musical America* (New York: Musical America Publishing, 1993)

Copland, Aaron and Vivian Perlis, *Success Story: Copland: 1900 Through 1942* (New York: St. Martin's, 1985)

Craft, Robert, *Stravinsky: Chronicle of a Friendship,* 1948-1971 New York: Knopf, 1972)

Craft, Robert, *A Stravinsky Scrapbook* (London: Thames & Hudson, 1983)

Crawford, Dorothy Lamb, *Evenings On and Off the Roof: Pioneering Concerts in Los Angeles: 1939-1971* (Berkeley: University of California Press, 1995)

Crawford, John C. and Dorothy L., *Expressionism in Twentieth Century Music* (Bloomington: Indiana University Press, 1993)

Faulkner, Robert R., *Hollywood Studio Musicians* (Lanham, Maryland: University Press of America,1985; originally Chicago, 1971)

Faulkner, Robert T., *Music on Demand: Composers and Careers in the Hollywood Film Industry* (New Brunswick: Transaction Books, 1983)

Griffiths, Paul, *Concise History of Avant-Garde Music: From Debussy to Boulez* (New York: Oxford University Press, 1978)

Griffiths, Paul, *Olivier Messiaen and the Music of Time* (Ithaca, New York: Cornell University Press, 1985

Griffiths, Paul, *Modern Music: The Avant-Garde Since 1945* (New York: Braziller, 1981)

Horowitz, Joseph, *Understanding Toscanini: How He Became an American Culture God and Helped Create a New Audience for Old Music* (Minneapolis: University of Minnesota Press, 1987)

Howard, Orrin, ed., *Festival of Music Made in Los Angeles* (Los Angeles: Los Angeles Philharmonic Association, 1981)

Libman, Lillian, *And Music at the Close: Stravinsky's Last Years* (New York: Norton, 1972)

Marquis, Alice Goldfarb, *Art Lessons* (New York: Basic Books, 1995)

McDonald, William F., *Federal Relief Administration and the Arts* (Columbus, Ohio: Ohio State University Press, 1969)

McWilliams, Carey, *Southern California: An Island on the Land* (Santa Barbara: Peregrine Smith, 1973)

Merrill-Mirsky, Carol, *"Exiles in Paradise,"* Catalogue of exhibition, Hollywood Bowl Museum (Los Angeles, 1991)

Palmer, Christopher, *The Composer in Hollywood* (New York and London: Marion Boyars, 1990)

Rabin, Carol Price, *Music Festivals in America* (Stockbridge, Massachuesetts: The Berkshire Traveller Press, rev. ed., 1983)

Rockwell, John, *All American Music: Composition in the Late Twentieth Century* (New York: Knopf,1983)

Slonimsky, Nicolas, *Perfect Pitch* (New York: Oxford University Press, 1988)

Slonimsky, Nicolas, *Music Since 1900,* 4th edition (New York: Scribners, 1971)

Slonimsky, Nicolas, *Supplement to Music Since 1900* (New York: Scribners, 1986)

Starr, Kevin, *Material Dreams: Southern California Through the 1920s* (New York: Oxford University Press, 1990)

Stravinsky, Igor and Robert Craft, *Conversations with Igor Stravinsky* (Berkeley: University of California Press, 1980)

Stravinsky, Igor, *Memories and Commentaries* (Berkeley: University of California Press, 1981)

Stravinsky, Igor, *Selected Correspondence,* ed. by Robert Craft (New York: Knopf, 1984)

Swan, Howard, *Music in the Southwest* (San Marino, California: Huntington Library, 1952)

Tawa, Nicholas E., *Art Music in the American Society* (Scarecrow Press: Metuchen, New Jersey, and London, 1987)

Tawa, Nicholas E., *Serenading the Reluctant Eagle* (New York: Schirmer, 1984)

Temianka, Henri, *Facing the Music* (New York: McKay, 1973)

Walter, Bruno, *Theme and Variations* (New York: Knopf, 1946)

Walter, Bruno, *Of Music and Music-Making* (New York: Norton, 1961)

Weaver, John D., *Los Angeles: The Enormous Village* (Santa Barbara: Capra Press, 1980)

Yates, Peter, *Twentieth Century Music* (New York: Pantheon, 1967)

Bibliography by Ellen Malino James